JESUS THE
PASTOR

FOREWORD BY
EUGENE H. PETERSON

JOHN W. FRYE

JESUS <u>THE</u>
PASTOR

LEADING OTHERS
IN THE CHARACTER
& POWER
OF CHRIST

ZondervanPublishingHouse
Grand Rapids, Michigan

A Division of HarperCollinsPublishers

Jesus the Pastor
Copyright © 2000 by John W. Frye

Requests for information should be addressed to:

ZondervanPublishingHouse
Grand Rapids, Michigan 49530

Library of Congress Cataloging-in-Publication Data

Frye, J. W.
    Jesus the pastor : leading others in the character and power of Christ / John W.
Frye ; foreword by Eugene H. Peterson.
      p.   cm.
    Includes bibliographical references.
    ISBN: 0-310-22995-2
    1. Jesus Christ—Person and offices.   2. Pastoral Theology.   I. Title.
BT205 .F79   2000
232.9'04—dc21   99-057937
                                            CIP

This edition printed on acid-free paper.

Interior design by Amy E. Langeler

Printed in the United States of America

99 00 01 02 03 04 05 /❖ DC/ 10 9 8 7 6 5 4 3 2 1

*To Julie, wife with the Shepherd's heart,
and to our daughters, Leah, Elisha, Lori, Shamar*

CONTENTS

FOREWORD

THOSE of us who are called to be Christian pastors find ourselves in a world in which we get to work daily and intensely with the Holy Scriptures and with human souls: these glorious Holy Scriptures; these glorious human souls. The Scriptures and the souls, in combination , provide a work world that is endlessly fascinating, a glorious world indeed.

Holy Scripture: We're assigned the task of studying and teaching and proclaiming these words of God, all that God reveals of himself in sentences and stories that transform our understanding of the world into a place and time charged with life-saving purpose.

Human souls: We're assigned the task of caring for these works of God, these image-of-God men and women who are the crowning achievement of God's creativity, guiding and accompanying them to live as they were intended, to "the praise of his glory."

But this glorious world is also an incredibly messy world. The Word of God revealed in the Scriptures is misquoted and maligned, distorted and denied, propagandized and polemicized. We pastors have our hands full disentangling it from the lies of the devil. And the work of God that we encounter in each soul is so sin-wounded and sin-scarred, whether beaten down by evil or bloated with pride, that it is difficult to discern what God had in mind back on the sixth day of creation when he pronounced it "very good." We pastors don't have it easy.

Whipsawed between the magnificent and the messy, it's no wonder that out of a sheer need for survival we look for an easy way out that will allow us to still keep our jobs. It's surprising how quickly options open up. Unfortunately, they all involve sidelining the work we took on in the first place, the Holy Scriptures and human souls. The big surprise is that when we start doing this—sidelining Scripture and souls—most people don't notice. It turns out that there are any number of ways of being religious without having much to do with God, whether in the Bible or the soul. And so we keep our jobs; better yet, more often than not we get promoted. But we also pay a terrible price: We lose the thrill that pulled us into this work in the first place; we lose the leisurely companionship with Jesus in which we were initiated as apprentices into the life of pastor.

And so it is always heartening to come across a pastor who stays on the job, refusing to abandon either the Scriptures or souls, and lives to tell the story. For me it is always a little like hearing the stories of people who have climbed Mount Everest or Annapurna or K2—*any* mountain, for that matter—and made it down again. You know that they were involved in absolutely breathtaking beauty; you also know that they negotiated incredible dangers.

John Frye is among such company. *Jesus the Pastor* is the account of his "climb." For pastoral work is an immersion in breathtaking beauty, the "greater things" that Jesus told us to expect as we follow him and work in his name (John 14:12). But it is also dangerous work, and the casualties are many. The pastoral vocation contributes more than its share of those who "have shipwrecked their faith" (1 Tim. 1:19). Experienced and reliable companions are essential as we do this work.

Because pastoral work is essentially creative work, a vocational participation in the work of the Creator Spirit, there are precious few procedural "how-to's" to guide us. Studying a text or mastering a set of skills doesn't get us very far. Creation is not copying—which means that there are about as many ways to be a pastor as there are pastors. At the same time, "creative" in pastoral work doesn't mean making it up as we go along; we follow Jesus, who makes all things new (Rev. 21:5). There is no way to be a Christian pastor that is not single-minded in following Jesus. John Frye recovers that focus for us and proves out to be a good companion in just such following.

EUGENE H. PETERSON
PROFESSOR EMERITUS OF SPIRITUAL THEOLOGY
REGENT COLLEGE, VANCOUVER, B.C.

PREFACE

OFTENTIMES the mean, old wolf would come to my pastoral door and say, "I'll huff and I'll puff and I'll blow your house down." Frightened by the threats, I wondered whether this vocation I've pursued, this calling I've heeded, was going to hold. Will the four walls weather the storm?

Two solid, reliable foundations on which to build strong walls of pastoral ministry that I learned from Eugene H. Peterson are (1) stay in one place and cultivate the pastoral field of souls, and (2) don't lose pastoral passion in the daily, sometimes tedious demands of pastoral work. Two other anchoring foundations are mentioned by Eugene Peterson in his gracious foreword to this book: the Holy Scriptures and human souls.

I have felt many times as if the walls would collapse and my best option was to get out of the house fast. Who needs the trauma or the tedium of the process of trying to see Christ formed in people? I would get to the place where I either really didn't like people anymore or I couldn't stand who I was as a person and as a pastor.

Little did I understand early on that all of it—triumph and tedium, magnificence and messiness—was part of the unfolding story of God's shaping my life as a pastor.

Somewhere among the shivering timbers I bumped into Jesus and discovered him to be more than Friend, King, Savior, and Lord. I bumped into Jesus the Pastor. He offered me his yoke—that is, he offered to share with me his skill as Shepherd. And, like the poet's road that diverged in the yellow wood, "that has made all the difference."

In this book I share my story as I began to explore the new trail. On this trail with me have been some very helpful companions.

I want to acknowledge first the tremendous and affirming people of Bella Vista Church, where I am privileged to pastor. When God placed me into the field of souls as a shepherd, he gave me a prime spot. In my years at Bella Vista Church the people have experienced some devastating messes and, through them, have discovered God's grace and love in new ways. They have also taken wings like eagles and flown magnificently. My story would not be possible without them.

I want to acknowledge my pastoral colleagues—John Raymond, a former Zondervan Publishing House marketing executive and now our executive pastor, who believed this project was worth pursuing and challenged me to do it; Wayne Squires, Tim Cosby, Denise VanEck, and Wendell and Rosemary Carlson, whose encouragement kept me going.

I want to acknowledge those who read and commented on early drafts of this book: Dr. Victor M. Matthews, professor emeritus of Grand Rapids Baptist Seminary; Wayne Benson, senior pastor of First Assembly of God in Grand Rapids; Rich Nathan, senior pastor of Columbus (Ohio) Vineyard Christian Fellowship; and good friend and writer, Ginger Sisson. Their kind comments only helped sharpen the message. Any dullness in the message is attributable only to me.

I want to acknowledge the band of students comprising the Christian Spirituality cohorts at Fuller Theological Seminary under Dr. Dick Peace and Dr. James Bradley. Among these men and women of God, my vision for pastoral work expanded and my appreciation for the beauty of the Body of Christ deepened. So thanks to Dick Peace, Jim, Peter, Anne, Dick Randall, John, Suzanne, Gloria, Ed, Wendy, Andy, Calvin, Mary, Bill, Blaine, Dan, and Steve. You all hold a special place in my heart. Peter, your "word" for me—"artist of the soul"—has done more than you imagine.

I am delighted that Zondervan Publishing House introduced me, a rookie, to the intricacies of producing a book. Thanks to Jack Kuhatschek, a tremendous editor and mentor, for allowing the manuscript to bolt out of the starting block; to Jim Ruark for his professional skills and wise advice; and to Stan Gundry, friend and former professor of mine, who offered his encouragement along the way.

From Julie, my wife for thirty years, and from my four admirable daughters, to whom I dedicate this book, I receive such freely given love. I often feel so undeserving. Through them, then, the Shepherd meets me most.

JOHN W. FRYE
ROCKFORD, MICHIGAN

INTRODUCTION

JESUS: THE MISSING PASTOR

SITTING on a tour bus packed with pastors and Christian businessmen weaving its way through the streets of Madras, India, I experienced one of those conversations that lives on long after the words stop. I was part of a group of pastors who were on a ten-day study tour learning about the culture, religions, and growing evangelical church of India. Next to me was an older, seasoned pastor of a large church in the heartland of America. We did not know each other, but suddenly we engaged in a brief and somewhat turbulent conversation that planted a seed thought in my mind—a thought that has matured over time, creating a new appreciation for my life as a pastor.

The conversation began abruptly when my fellow tourist turned to me and asked, "Who runs your church?"

"Excuse me?" I responded.

"Who runs your church?"

"We're a multiple elder-ruled church."

"What's *that* like?" he asked with a condescending smirk.

Noting his attitude, I began thinking, *Who is this guy and what is he after?* That he had never heard of elder rule just did not make sense. I responded, "Elder rule is where you have a plurality of men overseeing the life and ministries of the local church."

"Yeah, I know that, but who is *in charge* of your church?"

With this question I presumed that my seat partner wanted to talk a little ecclesiastical polity—you know, various views on how the church is governed. He must be after some friendly conversation to pass the time. So for conversation's sake, if he wanted to know about who was in charge of the church, I'd offer an idea.

"Jesus Christ is in charge of the church. He is the head."

"You have *him* on staff, do you?"

"Well, not exactly in the way you mean, but in a sense Jesus Christ is present."

"How's that?" he pursued.

"We believe that Jesus Christ, who is head of his body, the church, communicates his mind through the Spirit to those who serve as the elders, as the overseers of the church in its local expression. Jesus also communicates his presence by the gifts the Spirit gives to the church."

My traveling buddy got restless, seemingly exasperated. He looked at me as if I were some kind of pastoral alien.

"Yeah, but who runs the operation? Where does the buck stop? Do you run it? Does the buck stop with you?" he bellowed in my face.

I guess I am a little slow at times, but now it began to dawn on me. I realized that this touring pastor who was probing me with questions lived out an aggressive church management style like that of a powerful corporate CEO in the business arena.

Don't get me wrong—I believe we pastors can learn many valuable lessons from our brothers and sisters who slug it out in the marketplace. My seatmate, however, was frustrated because I was offering a different management approach to local church ministry from his autocratic style. I could tell that he had grown accustomed to and liked very much being the "man in charge" of his church. He was the one at the top of the church authority chain. His pointed questions were designed to let me know that *he* was the one who ran his church. The buck, when it stopped, stopped with him alone.

I must admit that I can get irritated quickly with church hotshots, and I felt like I was next to one. I thought, *So this guy, who—to quote that great theologian Clint Eastwood—is "a legend in his own mind," wants to know who runs the church operation, eh? Then let's go for it.*

I responded, "No, sir, the buck doesn't stop with me. And who runs the operation? you ask. I'm convinced that it is the Holy Spirit of God, who, as you put it, 'runs the church.' The Spirit alone empowers a pastor and his collection of diverse people to become and operate as a church—a church that is to be the living expression of Christ in the world. Elders and pastors may oversee the church, but in no way are they capable of 'running it.'"

Apparently I lost the man. He stared at me with a look of unbelieving scorn. In a huff he cut off eye contact and turned in his seat. I had failed his test of pastoral inquiry by not yielding any ground to his theology and practice of "running the church." His attitude and questions revealed his management style, and my answers revealed another.

> *The Spirit alone empowers a pastor and his collection of diverse people to become and operate as a church — a church that is to be the living expression of Christ in the world.*

I am not saying that his style is wrong, nor am I denying that Jesus Christ worked through this pastor to bring glory to God and to bring truth to people. Thinking back on that conversation, I realize that as I sat as a younger pastor next to an older one, holding as we did two different management styles, I really wanted to ruffle his feathers. I'll admit that I wanted the satisfaction of bursting what appeared to be his bubble of pontification.

CHANGING FOCUS

Years have passed since that brief, bristling verbal exchange. From the subterranean regions of my mind, an idea now emerges as a question: How seriously do pastors look to Jesus Christ as the one who shapes their vision and expression of pastoral ministry? While that short bus conversation concerned different ways to "run a church," the emerging idea that captivates my thinking is not primarily about church management, but about a much more serious matter. Could it be that we have focused on management to the neglect of the Messiah? Are we lecturing on leadership without truly consulting the Leader? Are we attending seminars on pastoring without giving serious consideration to the supreme Senior Pastor?

The purpose of the chapters that follow is to draw the Christian community's attention to (or back to) Jesus Christ as the Senior Pastor.

I strongly affirm that Jesus Christ is the head of his church (Col. 1:18) and is forever intensely interested in the people he bought with his blood.

The conversion of Saul of Tarsus (Acts 9) is a dramatic reminder of just how much the exalted Jesus Christ as head is vitally connected to the church, which is "his body." As Saul persecuted Christians, the resurrected Jesus confronted him with the graphic reality that Saul was persecuting him! "Saul, Saul, why do you persecute *me?*" (v. 4, italics mine). As pastors we must never forget Jesus' initial question to Saul. In that question we come face to face with the staggering truth of the living union between Jesus and his people.

I have often listened to pastors at conferences complain about all the sacrifices they make for their people. Sadly, they have many stories to tell about pouring out their lives among ungrateful people. Ministry weary and fatigued physically, they come to conferences hoping for one sure word that what they are doing with their lives is worth the pain. Yet, for all the sacrifices we pastors think we make, nothing we do or give up for the sake of our calling will ever compare with Jesus' self-giving life and his sacrificial death on the cross. With his own blood he purchased people for God. We will never do that.

> *Nothing we do or give up for the sake of our calling will ever compare with Jesus' self-giving life and his sacrificial death on the cross.*

I am writing this book about Jesus, the Senior Pastor. This concept is not new; it is, however, sadly missing from many discussions of pastoral ministry today. Grounded firmly in the bedrock of biblical revelation is the truth that Jesus is the Chief Shepherd. Our common English word *pastor* has made its way to us through Latin and is simply the semantic equivalent of the biblical word for "shepherd."[1] It is a title that Jesus wore gladly and redeemed by his life and ministry. The term *pastor (shepherd)* may be gutted of value in our culture (even in the evangelical culture), but never is it downplayed by Jesus or the New Testament writers. Jesus Christ is the supreme Shepherd and thus the ultimate Senior Pastor.

Both Jesus himself and Peter, one of Jesus' closest friends, voiced this pivotal pastoral reality. Jesus said, "I am the good shepherd. The good shepherd lays down his life for the sheep. . . . I am the good shepherd; I know my sheep and my sheep know me . . . and there shall be one flock and one shepherd" (John 10:11, 14, 16). Peter, in giving directives to his fellow elders, wrote: "Be shepherds of God's flock that is under your care. . . . And when the Chief Shepherd appears, you will receive the crown of glory that will never fade away" (1 Peter 5:2, 4).

The writer of Hebrews, after calling leaders and people to their mutual responsibilities within the believing community, pointed to Jesus Christ as the ultimate Pastor by describing him as "our Lord Jesus, that *great Shepherd* of the sheep" (Heb. 13:20, italics mine). Pastors and people are to look up and out from themselves to the ultimately effective pastor, Jesus Christ, our model and counselor.

With these clear biblical affirmations about Jesus as the Senior Pastor, why have pastors and churches not been driven to him as the central and controlling focus for the pastoral vocation and ministry in the local church? I am not saying that Jesus has been totally neglected; rather, he has been relegated to other dimensions of Christian and local church experience. Jesus is shoved into *our* shadows as we read our management books, do our cultural surveys, attend our leadership seminars, and applaud or criticize one another's endeavors.

In recent years, however, Jesus Christ, our Great Shepherd, has begun to emerge from the shadows, revealing his glorious presence and resuming his rightful place among our ministries. In these days of worldwide renewal, Jesus' name is once again being exalted to the highest place, and he is retaking his place as Pastor. Even so, practically speaking, Jesus goes unconsulted by pastors and churches today as the primary and ultimate focus of their calling. While we may lift Christ up as Savior, as we bow down to him as Lord, as we marvel at his offices of Prophet, Priest, and King, as we walk with him as Friend, we seem to ignore him as the supreme Senior Pastor.

As the pastoral vocation teeters on the brink of the new millennium, churches and the world will increasingly need undershepherds who are less like each other and increasingly more like Jesus, the Chief Shepherd. A new breed of pastors must step up and seize their calling, a calling that propels them to live and minister as Jesus him-self did.

> Churches and the world will increas-ingly need under-shepherds who are less like each other and increas-ingly more like Jesus, the Chief Shepherd.

As a pastor I know that my ministry peers are notoriously focused on management styles, leadership models, and "suc-cessful" churches and pastors as examples to follow. I and the church staff with whom I serve have focused on a good share of them ourselves.

I have attended at least forty different national, regional, and local pastors' conferences in my twenty years as a pastor. I have learned many helpful tips and have been inspired and encouraged. I have laughed and cried and have been strategically informed and powerfully challenged. I am not against pastors' conferences; I hope to attend many more as I continue in pastoral ministry.

Neither do I mean to be piously carping about our apparent fixa-tion on one another as pastors. Nor am I saying we have nothing to learn from one another at conferences or other gatherings. What really bothers me these days is the uneasy conscience I have over our neglect of Jesus Christ as Pastor in our vision and expression of pas-toral work.

My spirit is needled by questions like this: What promotes the obvious lack of any meaningful discussion or honest "shop-talk" among pastors about Jesus Christ as the Senior Pastor of the church? What accounts for our many intense (and often adversarial) conver-sations about the vast variety of *visible* shepherds on the church land-scape? Where is our embarrassment for the almost total absence of any serious dialogue about Christ, our *invisible*, yet highly competent, supreme Senior Pastor? Why is Jesus—the Pastor who is eminently capable of capturing our hearts, challenging our minds, and compe-tently training us for our calling—unconsulted by us?

What exegetical detour did we take to fixate almost solely on Paul, an apostle (not a pastor), and his letters to shape our pastoral work to the almost total neglect of Jesus and the Gospels?[2] Why have we neglected Jesus Christ, who was and is the Pastor of Pastors—a Pastor we are privileged to observe in action through reading the gospel records? These are the kinds of questions that make me uneasy and reveal my struggle.

MAKING JESUS OUR MENTOR

I want to encourage my fellow shepherds to return to the Lord Jesus Christ (even as I am trying to return to him) as our number one pastoral mentor. Like Nicodemus, the celebrated teacher of Israel, we need to sneak away in the night, meet with Jesus on the sly, and talk over with him our questions about how God does his work in the world.

I hope the story of my own journey—personally and pastorally—will ring true and draw them into a similar quest. I pray that they will experience, mysteriously and quietly, "deep calling to deep" in their souls. I hope that as undershepherds they will be increasingly attentive to the voice of their Chief Shepherd and Friend. As they do, they will experience a warm welcome home like a returning to their "first love."

Our renewed focus on Jesus as Senior Pastor will result in a lot of extraneous clergy baggage, picked up over the years and associated with our pastoral calling, being gladly jettisoned. Baggage picked up from the social and psychological sciences and public relations industry will be recognized as expendable or at least not as urgently needed as supposed. Cheap pastoral gimmickry on how to pack out the church or fill up the Sunday school will be seen for what it really is—gimmickry.

Am I suggesting that pastors ignore one another in our renewed admiration of and attention to Christ as our pastoral model? No, but I am calling us to an intentional and honest admission and correction of our embarrassing neglect of Christ.

To spark some interest in conversations about Jesus Christ as Senior Pastor, I offer this book. As you read you will observe that I am revealing some of my own life transformation as a man who had to face the dark side of being from a "broken home." I tell about my theological shift from a trained skepticism about the Spirit and his gifts to the church to a warm appreciation for and acceptance of all his gifts—a shift that may delight some and puzzle others. I tell some stories about pastoral work, and I acknowledge some others who have guided me. I do some reflecting on Bible texts as they relate to Jesus Christ as Chief Shepherd, hopefully with an encouraging invitation to pastors to find renewal and perseverance in him as they fulfill their high calling.

The controlling idea of this book is that Jesus' undershepherds—pastors—are to be like their Chief Shepherd both in character and in ministry. I ask that you imagine that we are sitting at the table sipping coffee and dialoguing on matters of mutual pastoral concern. We may not see eye to eye on all that is discussed, but because we respect one another we will listen. The supreme focus will be Jesus Christ, the one who unites us, and not the secondary issues that separate us. About Jesus we agree. In him we are bonded as brothers and sisters. My hope is that we will fix our eyes and our conversation on Christ.

JESUS THE PASTOR

WATCHING HIM WORK

"JOHN, watch me."

From the sixth-grade year of my life until now I have had a step-father. His name is Neal. He is a good, energetic man who has taught me much about life. In fact, Neal's method of teaching me has greatly influenced my life as a pastor. I didn't always appreciate his training in my younger years, but I now see that he was shaping me for the demands of real life over the long haul.

Neal is an exceptional mechanic. If there is such a thing as the spiritual gift of mechanic (and maybe there is), Neal has it. When I was in junior high and high school, Neal operated a Mobil gas station in Waukegan, Illinois, that had two service bays and a car wash. I was hired to pump gas and learn something about cars. While I missed a lot of activities in high school because I was needed at the station, I also had some exciting, knuckle-skinning times around some pretty hot cars—Corvettes, stock cars for racing, dragsters, hemi-heads, the whole ball of grease. I hung out in a teenage boy's dream world.

I remember a day when a car came in misfiring, the engine having quiet spasms. Neal took a long screwdriver, placed the sharp end on the valve cover of the running engine, then leaned over and put his ear on the screwdriver handle and listened. He told the driver to turn off the engine and told me that we had to tear the engine down and do something with the pistons and crankshaft bearings. I remember thinking, *How does he know that?*

With the engine out, torn down, and inspected, I discovered that Neal's diagnosis was on target. What I had to learn by grimy inspection and guided instruction, Neal just seemed to intuit. I was often amazed.

Neal's primary way of teaching was this: "John, watch me. Watch what I do as I take things apart. Watch how I fix them, and then watch how I do the reassembly." I did—many, many times. I saw intake manifolds, heads (even some old flatheads), engine blocks (straight 6, V-8, and 4-cylinder), camshafts, crankshafts, pistons, valves, valve lifters, push rods, carburetors, clutches, fly wheels, transmissions (standard and automatic), and on and on. After some time, I was able, as a high school kid, to overhaul an engine by myself. I felt the rush of incredibly good feelings and a sense of anticipation in turning on the ignition to an engine that I had personally rebuilt from its hundreds of separated parts. Having repaired and reassembled them according to specs, the thrill of hearing the engine fire into operation with a deafening roar was better than fireworks on the Fourth of July. We almost always connected the exhaust system *after* we heard the ear-ripping sound of internal combustion at work. We were way, way ahead of "Tim the tool man."

"John, watch me." I hear Jesus saying this to me, now that I am a pastor, just as Neal did when I was a budding, young mechanic. Jesus offers on-the-job training. Did you know that the Old Testament word for "understanding" *(bin)* is built on the root word "to separate (in pieces)"?[1] Every time I tore an engine down and separated its components to discover why it wasn't running right, I was working with the process involved in the art of understanding.

What has gone wrong with human beings? Why don't we function well? What happened, for example, that caused me to "throw a rod" or "blow a gasket" in my early forties? We need to "understand," "to separate the parts" and see what needs repairing. Jesus is the supreme repairer of the human life. Nothing is hidden from his eyes or ears. He takes the shattered and creates *shalom*, takes the wrecked and creates wholeness.

God has made it possible for anyone to watch Jesus. We have the record of Jesus' life in action captured in the four Gospels—Gospels that vibrate with his high-velocity teachings and his supercharged, compelling actions.

The Son of God came to earth for many reasons—to demonstrate that he was the prophesied Messiah of Israel, to reveal the Father, to initiate the new covenant, to reconcile a rebellious universe to God, to take away the sins of the world. Jesus also came as the Chief Shepherd to pastor. Let's fire up our imaginations and take a creative look at Jesus in the act of pastoring.

> God has made it possible for anyone to watch Jesus. We have the record of Jesus' life in action captured in the four Gospels.

"John, watch me."

COMING TO JESUS

The night is quiet and still. Pungent smoke from the fires used for cooking the evening meals hangs low over Jerusalem. Jesus is sitting alone on a bench, leaning against the low roof wall. Waiting under an open black sky so full of stars, it's like he could reach up and scoop them into his hands to make a snowball. A dog barks in the distance, and soon Jesus hears quick footsteps on the outside stairway leading to the roof. A man, wealthy and intelligent looking, appears at the top of the stairs and looks around. Seeing Jesus, he approaches and sits beside him on the bench.

The man speaks quietly as he glances furtively around the rooftop. "Thank you, Rabbi, for being willing to see me under these unusual circumstances. I must be extremely cautious about being seen with you because of who I am and what I represent."

"I know, Nicodemus," Jesus whispers in response. "I am pleased we could meet, even if so secretly. Why did you want to see me?"

"We know—at least some of us in the Sanhedrin do—that you come from God. The things you say and the miraculous things you do can only be explained if God is with you. We who are responsible for the teaching in Israel are trying to make sense of the uproar you have stirred in our nation, but we end up embroiled in fierce debates over you. A few of us argue that we need to give you a fair hearing, others think you are very dangerous, and still others do not know what to decide. So, Rabbi, I wanted to meet you face to face and talk, even if under the cloak of night."

A gentle breeze blows by, and the hazy blanket of smoke over the housetops shifts, dancing into invisibility. Silence, extended and tangible, becomes third party to the conversation. Finally, Jesus breathes deeply and speaks.

"Nicodemus, I am about new beginnings. Unless you and the others start fresh—that is, are actually born all over again into the kingdom of God—you'll miss it completely."

"What do you mean 'born again'? That's impossible for me, for any man my age."

Jesus chuckled and said, "Think about it. You'll get the idea when the Spirit helps you understand the parallels between the spiritual realm and the natural realm. These parallels are all around you. You have to have a new beginning. Consider, for example, the breezes that blow by. Where do they come from? Where do they go? No one can tell. But you can see and feel the effects as the wind passes by. Likewise, the kingdom of God comes as the Spirit brushes against human lives."

"I don't understand."

Smiling, Jesus said, "You, Nicodemus? You don't understand? You are the teacher of Israel. You, of all people, must understand. You can trust me because, like you said, I have come to you from God. I am trying to help you and anyone who will listen. By speaking of the divine and timeless in ordinary, everyday terms, I intend to usher in God's reign. It doesn't take a scholar to understand; it takes a believer. Ages ago when many of our people were dying of snake-bite venom in the wilderness rebellion, Moses lifted up the symbol of a brass snake on a pole. People simply looked at it and their lives were miraculously spared. Listen. I will be lifted up, too, Nicodemus, and whoever will look to and trust me will receive the life of God's eternal kingdom."

This is an imaginative conversation but not far-fetched. On that night and in that talk, Jesus caused the wind of the Spirit to blow Nicodemus's way. Nicodemus brushed up against God, and he wasn't the same afterward. Later in John's gospel we see Nicodemus taking a gutsy stand for Jesus in the face of hostile peer opposition. Nicodemus argued the minority point that his colleagues were being unjust in prejudging Jesus without a fair hearing (John 7:50–52). Then later still, after Jesus' death, it is Nicodemus who, with Joseph of Arimathea, requests that Pilate release Jesus' body for proper Jewish burial (John 19:39–40).

TEACHING OR EXPERIENCING?

I like this conversation in John 3 because I, too, am a teacher—a pastor-teacher. Although I am not on the scale of a Nicodemus, I am responsible for the spiritual formation of a congregation. I want to "keep in step with the Spirit," to hoist my sails in the face of the Spirit's windy visitations, to see *in experience* the present kingdom of God. Like Nicodemus, I need to be reminded by Jesus himself that in kingdom matters I am not in control and never will be and that it is a privilege to be a teacher. *Teaching about* the kingdom, even great Nicodemus-level teaching, is not the same as *experiencing* the kingdom.

Oswald Chambers points me toward anticipating kingdom newness on a daily basis when he writes: "Being born again by the Spirit is an unmistakable work of God, as mysterious as the wind, and as surprising as God Himself. We don't know where it begins—it is hidden away in the depths of our soul. Being born again from above is an enduring, perpetual, and eternal beginning. It provides a freshness all the time in thinking, talking, and living—a continual surprise of the life of God."[2]

Jesus, as *my* Pastor, is waiting. He will meet me in the night away from the noise and conflict of adversarial views of ministry. Not everyone agrees these days, just as they didn't agree in Jesus' day, about how God is at work in the world. He knows that I get confused. He knows that this bewildering confusion can cause me to become tentative and guarded rather than courageous and daring. He wants me to be clearheaded about the most incredible invasion of human history—the inbreaking of the reign of God—in my time, in my state, in my church, in my very life. So he will hear me out and tell me straight what I need to hear to succeed as a pastor who is hungry for the Spirit and for the Spirit's work.

"John, watch me."

Once again there is no wind. But now it is fiercely hot as the sun blazes at noon. The horizon ripples in the heat as Jesus, on his way to Galilee, decides to do the unexpected and risky thing. "I must do it." He heads north through Samaria, breaking the protocol of good Jews who bypass Samaria by going north on the east side of the Jordan River.

As Jesus and his disciples near Sychar, the disciples are sweating, but not just from the Palestinian sun. They are fretting, heated up emotionally because they are on unclean ground, worrying over their proximity to a very unclean people—the Samaritans. Everything that has been ingrained in them as good Jewish men is violated with every step they take. As Jews they feel superior. As Jews in Samaria they feel threatened.

Jesus is tired and thirsty, so he stops to rest in the shade of trees around Jacob's well. The disciples, hungry from the walk, argue and worry about what Jesus could possibly be up to in traveling through this "no man's land." On the way into town to get food, they strategize "damage control" for themselves and Jesus, barely noticing a woman avoiding them as she hurries out of town.

The woman has a water pot. She rushes as quickly as the heat will allow, hoping to fill her jar and get back to town before other women of the village come later to the well in the cool of the day. She comes at noon so that she can come alone. The heat and the rush cause her to sweat, and she wishes the sweat would wash from her soul her searing shame and inner pain as the moisture leaves her body.

Filling her jar and sitting down in the cool shade, the woman decides to rest a moment before she scurries back to Sychar. She leans against the rough bark of a tree and closes her eyes, resting a moment to catch her breath. The rest feels so good.

Startled, she jerks her head toward the voice of a stranger saying, "Give me a drink of water." She had not noticed the man, clearly a Jew by appearance, also resting in the shade of a nearby tree.

Shame creates unusual skill in people. Instantly she sizes up the situation. All the known factors that separate her from others, especially from a Jewish man, flood her thinking. Shame makes her quick on her feet, planning the route of her swift retreat. She says to Jesus the expected thing, the culturally appropriate thing, the thing that will release her back into her painfully isolated life.

"How is it that you, a Jew, ask the likes of me, a Samaritan and a woman at that, for a drink? I know and you know that I am way out of bounds to you and your kind."

Remarkably Jesus does not accept her socially and politically correct answer, and so he does not release her into a quick get-away. He, shockingly enough, continues to engage her in what unfolds to be a revelatory, if not ruffled, conversation. Using words as wrenches, Jesus expertly dismantles her soul, finds the bad part, does the repair by revealing himself as Messiah, and sends her, overhauled and firing on all eight cylinders, back into town.

With Nicodemus it was wind; with this woman it is water. Taking the ordinary thing—water—and an ordinary need—thirst—Jesus swings open the gates of the kingdom of heaven and ushers the Samaritan woman into God's presence. By his actions she is now tuned up as a worshiper of the Father in spirit and truth.

The disciples come back, survey the scene of Jesus conversing in burning daylight with a *woman*, a *Samaritan* woman at that, and continue to feel really jumpy about the whole situation. Jesus refuses the meal they have brought him and instead speaks about food they know nothing about. "Doing the will of God my Father is my food," he tells them.

MASTERING SMALL TALK

What do we discover about Jesus as a pastor in this conversation with the Samaritan woman? Jesus treated her the way our loving God and Father treats everyone: he accepted and respected her *as a person*. He did not treat her as women were then treated; he treated her as a person. He did not treat her as Jews treated Samaritans; he treated her as a person. He did not treat her as a heretic; he treated her as a person. Dr. Victor Matthews, a friend and theologian, says, "Jesus gave the Samaritan woman her rightful place in his life. Her rightful place was as a human being, a person made in the image of God. She had the right to be treated as a person. That is always the way God in his love treats us."[3]

What do you get when you take a highly influential Jewish teacher in Israel and an immoral, skeptical Samaritan woman and factor in Jesus? You get phenomenal models for pastoral conversation at both ends of the social scale. How can I as a pastor protect my belief that *each individual is made in the image of God and, therefore, has worth* from becoming pious cliché? I guard this vital truth each time I receive persons, no matter who they are and where they are, into my life and engage them *on their terms* in a respectful and hopefully redemptive, but never contrived, conversation. We must become masters of ordinary "small talk" if we want to be good pastors.[4] *Heilsgeschichte* (salvation-history) comes in talk about simple things like wind and water, not in heady talk about Hebrew scrolls and Greek parchments.

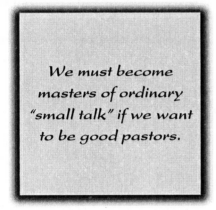

We must become masters of ordinary "small talk" if we want to be good pastors.

As I read thoughtfully through John's gospel or Luke's, I hear Jesus saying, "Watch me, John. Watch me treat every person with respect even if that respect carries the sting of rebuke or brings a response of hostile rejection. I write off no one automatically, but I count no one in automatically either. I respect the individual freedom of the human being to choose life or death. And I offer myself as life."

A businessman in the church wanted to meet and talk, so we decided to meet for lunch at a local restaurant. With lunch almost over and following small talk about his work and his wife and kids, he took a deep breath and confessed, "John, I'm homosexual."

Because I knew him and his family and because I respected him as a person, I was deeply rocked by his confession. I was sitting face to face with a person who confided in me the most agonizing struggle in his life. It was (and is) also one of the most volatile issues facing the Christian community.

"John, watch me."

This man and I met over many lunches, and he told me his story. I learned about his dysfunctional family of origin, of others in his family who were gay, of his difficulties relating to his wife, of his lapses into the sexual practice that shredded his soul and compounded his guilt, of his searingly disappointing trek through the evangelical community's best counseling efforts, of his solace and acceptance in the religious gay community.

We discussed the Bible and what it teaches about homosexuality. He gave me literature written by biblical scholars that argued for the legitimacy of loving, committed gay relationships. I read the material but could not agree with the conclusions that argued for sanctioning same-sex relationships. I shared my negative evaluations of the material openly, at times forcefully, but always with a deep respect for the person who had confided his awful torment to me.

This man continued to come to our church until he was transferred through his business out of the state. Always he knew that I accepted him and respected him as a person. Homosexuality was not an issue or a debate for me; it was an incarnate struggle in a person with a name. I tried to remember that I was not meeting with *a homosexual*. I was meeting and pastoring *a person* who struggled with homosexuality. He knew and felt that distinction, and he received me as friend and pastor, though he did not always like what I brought to our conversations.

With the help of another friend in the church, I have thought about my conversations with that businessman struggling with homosexuality. A friend I respect highly pressed me to really think about the parallels between Jesus' relationship and conversation with the woman at the well and my conversations with the man in the restaurant. Did I secretly want to "win" in our discussions about biblical morality more than I wanted my struggling friend to authentically know the life-changing love of an almighty God revealed in the person of Christ?

How much of an issue did Jesus make out of the woman at the well's marital history? How much time did he spend defining and defending God's moral code regarding marriage? When Jesus did reveal his knowledge of her repetitive moral failures, the woman acknowledged his penetrating insight as a prophet and then quickly changed the subject. What did Jesus do? He went with the flow. He didn't drag her back to her sordid moral state and try "to set her straight." He continued to respect her, even to love her, as a person. He saw her, even with her moral failures, as a potential worshiper of his Father.

I have not always been able to keep my ego as a pastor from tangling up knotty *issues* (like homosexuality) with struggling *people*. In my valiant attempts at times to "defend the faith," I have trampled on the lives of those whose struggles are both serious and sinful, yet who may, nonetheless, qualify in Christ to be my fellow worshipers of God. Jesus didn't offer the woman a restatement of the Mosaic moral law, he offered himself. She needed first and foremost a hero and Savior, the Messiah, not moral lessons on the sanctity of marriage.

My friend told me about a Bible study she led for people in the entertainment industry. She related that these people were not known for either their Bible knowledge or their commendable morality. The study was based on the Gospel of John.

One woman in the group was living with her male friend. The person of Jesus Christ as revealed in John's gospel captivated this woman. She received Christ as her Savior yet continued to live in violation of God's Word. My friend could have confronted the woman—her new sister in Christ—about her violation of the biblical moral code, but she didn't. She continued to love the woman and to introduce Jesus and God's Word to her.

Over time the Spirit used both my friend's accepting love and the Word's life-changing power to convince the woman that her lifestyle was wrong. *On her own* the woman made the choice to align her life with God's call to moral purity. My friend didn't have to win the morality battle. She, like Jesus, treated the woman with loving respect while believing that the Spirit and the Word would do their work.

Issues are issues. People are people. Issues need to be addressed. People need to be loved. Keeping out of the hurtful tangle of mixing people and issues takes a prolonged gaze at Jesus. He is the Master at keeping out of the ego-driven, moralistic, tangled mess that we often, with the best of intentions, make.

DAZED OR AMAZED?

We have "watched" Jesus with two individuals, but what about large audiences? How did Jesus pastor "congregations"? Once again, the Gospels provide us with "footage" of Jesus in action. Any cursory reading of the Gospels reveals that crowds of people were regularly amazed by Jesus' teaching and by his actions (Mark 1:22, 27; 2:12). Common people heard him gladly.

Sometimes I feel that my congregation is more dazed than amazed when I get done speaking. What can Jesus teach me when it comes to pastoring at the congregational, Sunday-morning-service level of contact?

As I am thinking about this question and about what we can learn from Jesus the Pastor, I feel like we're at the edge of the ocean and I'm scooping up a thimble of water, saying, "Here.

> *Issues are issues. People are people. Issues need to be addressed. People need to be loved.*

Take this. This is the ocean." This topic of Jesus as Pastor will occupy our minds and hearts for a long time. Like the ocean, the subject is wide and deep, but at least a thimbleful is a start.

"John, watch me."

When I think of Jesus the Pastor and crowds, one word comes to mind: story. Jesus the Pastor was a storyteller who told down-to-earth stories about everyday experiences and ordinary things. Some pastors are bothered by the fact that Jesus told stories. I, however, am now intrigued by it.

Storytelling is certainly one practice that might have Jesus ejected from many of our evangelical pulpits. Why didn't Jesus spend more time "exegeting Isaiah 53" or expounding the intricacies of Daniel's seventieth week? Why didn't the Son of God, the most brilliant human being to ever live, solve the mysteries of God and evil or at least explain who the "sons of God" were in Genesis 6:1–4? Why did he spend so much time talking about earthy things like dirt and seed, flowers and birds, fish and nets, pearls and pigs? He created characters like stubborn judges, rebellious sons, lazy workers, callous religious leaders, compassionate outcasts, and risqué women. So let's be frank and just ask it: Why wasn't Jesus a good Bible expositor?

Jesus modeled for us what people deeply long to know: Is God somehow involved in the day-to-day details of our sometimes happy, sometimes hard lives? So Jesus, out of his discipline of creative meditation, spun stories. His stories brought people to what ancient Celtic theologians called the "thin places," those places where the divine and human connect, where the natural and supernatural meet. Jesus believed in a "God-bathed and God-permeated world" (to use Dallas Willard's phrase from *The Divine Conspiracy*) so that everything around him and us might bring us to a thin place, the threshold of an entirely new life in another realm of existence—the kingdom of God.

Stories primarily do two things.[5] First, they engage the imagination. They trigger our thinking. By telling stories, Jesus treated people, even the common, poor folk of the land, as thinkers. Jesus believed that his stories would stimulate the presence and the power of the imagination of his hearers. With the Spirit's revealing work, common people would find themselves encountering the living God and facing Jesus' challenge to make life-altering decisions.

Sadly, the religious leaders of Jesus' day didn't believe common people could think. Nor did these religious guardians care about the imagination. Huddled in their studious conclaves, the religious leaders thought themselves to be brilliant.

Second, stories invite participation. Once the story is told and the imagination engages and the Spirit works, people are brought to decision. Where am I in this story? Am I in it at all? What will I do to finish the story? Consider the end of Luke 15—the parable of the prodigal son. Did the self-absorbed and self-righteous older brother heed his father's words or not? Jesus doesn't tell us. The story is not brought to closure. It doesn't come full circle. Why? Because we are pulled into the story and pressed to create the ending with our choices. Jesus was brilliant.

Now, lest those exegetical pastors who are reading toss this book aside, let me add that I enjoy doing exegetical work. Good biblical exegesis is valuable and necessary. We are bound to "correctly handle the word of truth" (2 Tim. 2:15). But with Jesus as our model, we are bound to be good storytellers as well as good expositors if we truly want to pastor crowds the way Jesus did. Methodist church historian Leonard Sweet, discussing the making of the DreamWorks film *Prince of Egypt*, declares "story-tellers will be the leaders of the new millennium."[6]

A good story will fire the imagination and draw others into the action as participants. Jesus trusted the human being, fallen and common, with an ability to hear, discern, and decide for God on the basis of homespun stories. Jesus did not presume to do others' thinking for them. He treated them as thinking, feeling, and deciding beings. Will we pastors in this age be like Jesus and do the same?

On the fifth Sunday of November 1997, Tony and I stood before the congregation and administered the Lord's Table. I presented the bread and Tony presented the cup. The Lord's Table, representing Jesus' reconciling work, had special meaning for Tony and me and our church. It was truly a miracle Sunday.

Six years earlier Tony had been on the church staff, and I, along with the other elders, decided that Tony, for his own good, needed to be fired. The hard decision was made. Tony and his wife, Amy, and his family were devastated. Many people in the church were stunned.

About five years later, Tim, our new pastor of worship ministries, began serving on staff. As the new guy who had no knowledge of Tony, Tim kept hearing in conversations about "the decision to fire Tony." The decision, while accepted by most people, never really *found rest* in their souls. Tim, who has the New Testament gift of prophecy, believed that God wanted to do something new, perhaps even stupendous, with the whole "Tony situation."

I was forced to wrestle again with all the issues of the "Tony situation." While admitting that the process followed in firing Tony was wrong, I always defended the decision itself. But now God was bringing the decision back to me unsolicited. Had firing Tony truly been the right thing to do? Having apologized to Tony for the process, did God want me to apologize for the decision itself?

I asked myself, "What keeps you defending a decision that clearly hurt Tony and his family and that has never settled in the souls of many people in the church?" One word came to mind: pride. Years earlier, in the days of the process and decision, my ego had become caught up in the relational machinery.

Tim challenged me with the question, "John, what do you have to lose by apologizing to Tony for the decision itself?" I thought seriously about that question, going deep down to where I had buried the decision. I saw the bedrock of pride, and suddenly a new light blazed in me. I responded, "Nothing. I have nothing to lose, but I have a brother to gain."

With much prayer, Tim and I, along with another staff member, Wayne, decided to call Tony and Amy and set the reconciling process in motion. I would apologize to Tony. We set a date for the visit. I would call Tony to make the arrangements.

On the very day that Tim, Wayne, and I discussed and decided on the date, I received a call at the church—*from Tony*. Tony told me that he was in a men's Bible study and that he was being moved by the Spirit to reconcile with me and with the church regarding his bad feelings. I told Tony how the Lord was working in the others and in me and how I was about to call him to get together to talk. Now Tony was stunned by the Spirit's work. We were both in tears.

We did meet. Tony and Amy, Tim, Wayne, and I met in Tony's home. We sat at his table and related how the Lord was at work in us. Tony and Amy shared deep hurts and grievances. Tears were dropping all around the table. I apologized to Tony for the decision that had brought so much harm, darkness, and distance into his life and family.

In one of the most significant moments of my pastoral ministry, with a basin and towel, I washed Tony's feet, confessing my sins against him and his family. Wayne washed Amy's, confessing his sorrow over all the anguish we had brought to her husband, to her, and to her children. Tony and Amy told us later that they literally felt the love of Christ during the washing and confession.

Tony asked to be publicly welcomed back into and reconciled with the church. We said, "Done deal." Some weeks later, on the fifth Sunday of November 1997, I publicly apologized to Tony and Amy and welcomed them back into the church. Tony told the church about his own prolonged "dark night of the soul" and of God's restoring work in him. The church felt God's peace. Together Tony and I ministered the Lord's Table. One cup. One loaf. One body.

Jesus is still telling awesome stories.

How many stories have you heard in which a fired church staff member was reconciled back to the church that fired him? Please understand me. I am not bragging. Still stunned even as I write this, I am simply telling a story. It is a Jesus story—not a John story, Tony story, or a Wayne, Tim, or church story. Jesus is still telling awesome stories. Tony and I and the others were just happily chosen to be in this one.

DESCENDING INTO GREATNESS

Having observed Jesus with individuals and with crowds, perhaps we should now ask, "How did Jesus pastor his closest friends, his chosen disciples?" Reading the Gospels reveals that Jesus had some specific intentions as he shepherded that small group, that little platoon of twelve people. At times he was deeply thrilled and satisfied with them; at others times he was aggravated and disappointed. Yet at all times he loved them passionately, including Judas Iscariot, the traitor. Let's take a look at how Jesus shepherded the leader of the Twelve, Peter, son of Zebedee, at a critical moment in Jesus' life—the night he was betrayed by Judas into the hands of his enemies.

"Watch me, John."

In Jerusalem, on this holy night of Passover, the disciples' short tempers flared, and once again they scorched each other with heated words. During the meal, Jesus had mentioned something about the fulfillment of the kingdom. The way Jesus spoke and what he said made the disciples sense that this night was indeed like no other. They had also begun to do the math—there were only two seats next to King Jesus in his kingdom and there were twelve of them.

If we were able to play a tape recording of that boisterous argument, it would be hard to miss Peter's voice drowning out the others as each disciple began to fiercely vindicate himself as worthy of one of those two seats. This dispute was old news to Jesus. He had already confronted their competitive quest to outrank each other when the triumphant kingdom of God was ushered in. Now, on this last night with the disciples before his death, he had to do it again.

Jesus quietly withdrew from the table as the disciples continued arguing. Jesus let his outer garment, his seamless robe, drop to the floor. He went over to the entryway of the upper room and took the servant's basin and towel and came back to his friends. When he started washing Matthew's feet, Matthew suddenly dropped out of the debate. Then Andrew, and Philip, and Thomas quieted down as Jesus washed their feet. Soon all were quiet except Peter. Peter—he was in rare form. With his adrenaline flowing, he was willing even to argue with Jesus over the footwashing. "I'll show these rivals and Jesus, too, that I'm someone to reckon with. I am a leader. One of those seats in the kingdom has my name on it." As Jesus approached Peter with the basin and towel, Peter spoke out firmly, "Take a break, Jesus, you'll never wash my feet. Period."

Squaring up face to face, Jesus looked Peter straight in the eyes. "Is that right, Peter? You're arguing for a throne, aren't you? Let me tell you something, Peter. If I don't wash your feet, you won't get near a throne or me. As a matter of fact, you won't get anything in my kingdom, tough guy. Never say 'never.' So, tell me, Peter, what's your decision?"

After the footwashing Jesus reminded the disciples how people without God in the world continually do what they had just been doing—clamor for power over others. "My kingdom is not marked by competitive power, but by compassionate servanthood. You want to be great. And I want you to be great too. But the greatest in my kingdom is least of all. You all are destined to be leaders—leaders like me, who comes as the servant of all. In my kingdom, you descend into greatness."

"Tonight you were once again trying hard to convince each other of your claim to greatness in the kingdom. But I know that tonight each one of you will scatter like sheep, deserting me as I am betrayed into the hands of evil men. Truly great leaders of mine discover bravery in their brokenness, uncover strength in their weakness, and forge a commitment in the face of their cowardice. This is puzzling to you, I know, but soon you will know exactly what I am talking about."

Having accepted the footwashing, Peter is still struggling within himself. He is not agreeing with Jesus at all. He cannot imagine himself deserting Jesus. He has heard this servant-leader pep talk before, and still it gets past him. "I am a brave man. Jesus needs to know it."

"Lord, I make mistakes. Lots of them. But, Lord, one thing I won't do is cut and run. If need be, when the enemy comes, I'll be at your side. If you die, I'll die with you—tonight. If you go down, I go down too. We're a team, Lord." The other disciples chime in, agreeing with Peter and affirming their loyalty to Jesus as well, even in the face of death.

"Peter, Peter, how I love you. Love tells the truth. Hear me, Peter. This very night the Enemy desires to blow you away like chaff from grains of wheat. I am on my knees before the Father praying for you, Peter. Tonight, rather than dying with me, you will deny me three times before the rooster crows. You are going to head down a very dangerous, painful, but necessary road. You will get turned around, however; and when you do, come back with what you have learned and put iron in the resolve of these friends of ours."

Peter fulfilled to the letter everything Jesus predicted. The others also fled into the shadows when Jesus was arrested. They did what the Shepherd said they would do: they deserted him. Peter, ticking like a Swiss watch, denied Jesus the third time just as the rooster crowed.

Once again, as earlier in the evening, Jesus looked Peter squarely in the eyes. No words were needed now. Peter's wide and wild eyes shouted, "Jesus! Just like you said, I've failed." Jesus' eyes, rimmed with tears, whispered, "Peter, just like I said, I've prayed." Then the fearless, brave, throne-seeking Peter broke. He wept bitterly, his tears liquid reminders that he had nothing in himself, absolutely nothing to bring to the battlefield that could help him win.

The pastoral ministry of Jesus to the Twelve was a constant endeavor to convince them that the "poor in spirit" receive the kingdom. Day after day for the time that Jesus and the Twelve lived together, Jesus wanted them to catch the vision of a God-saturated world. Jesus persisted in the face of their meager, ego-driven aspirations to lift their vision higher, to sweep them into God's forceful kingdom powers and purposes. He continually pried their fingers off of their small ideas about God and people, and, then, into their *empty* hands he placed the keys to God's kingdom.

Pastorally, Jesus pointed them down the road of pain. In the fiery furnace of personal failure, the impurities of self-reliance were burned away. It is the pain of facing deep, personal emptiness, inner nothingness, that convinces Jesus' leaders of the fact that apart from him, they can do nothing. I wish it weren't so, but I too have been down that necessary road.

"Watch me, John."

Since we have seen Jesus doing pastoral ministry with individuals, crowds, and the Twelve, we are ready now to explore in an extended way some ideas about Jesus and the vocation of pastoring. I love to pastor, but it has not always been so. What has changed me? I am eager to let you know.

JESUS AND PASTORING

REDEFINING THE PASTORAL VOCATION

As most pastors do, I like books. One book in my library that is a prized possession is by Eugene H. Peterson titled *Five Smooth Stones for Pastoral Work*. This book is valuable to me for two reasons. First, the book's content caused a continental shift in my understanding of the pastoral task. Second, my copy is autographed with these words:

> *For John,*
>
> *Sharing the life of Christ in the work of pastor—meeting you at Spring Arbor!*
>
> *Eugene H. Peterson, 24 June 1987*

I was stunned the first time I read *Five Smooth Stones*. I find myself rereading it periodically and saying under my breath, "Where have I been all these years?" My reaction is caused by Peterson's steady, drumbeat reminder that authentic pastoral work is not grounded in current trends or social sciences, but in ancient truths and scriptural personalities. Peterson painstakingly sinks a shaft into the deep strata of biblical revelation[1] and mines precious metal from which to forge a resilient vision of the pastoral calling. Have we been seduced into thinking that our priority is to be "in touch with our times" more than being immersed in biblical truth?

As a Bible college and seminary graduate, I am deeply thankful for my training for ministry. I sat under genuinely godly and amazingly competent teachers in two highly commendable theological schools. Yet I must confess that at no time in my training was I ever given a coherent, Bible-based vision of pastoral work similar to what is in *Five Smooth Stones*. I am not complaining, but I am wondering why this is so. I received a coherent "systematic theology" but a very random, unsystematic pastoral theology. My seminary training was in the early seventies when theologians and pastors were "rethinking the church," and maybe being a well-trained pastor slipped through the cracks during the intense pursuit of answering, "What is a local church anyway?"

Through the years I have had to sew together my own patchwork quilt of pastoral work. With snatches of verses from this text and that, with pieces of advice from this prominent pastor and that ministry workshop, from paragraphs in this leadership book and that management seminar, I created the fabric of personal pastoral practice. I carried my concealed fabric from one pastors' conference to the next, and when I heard something "new" or something I was told that I couldn't be a competent pastor without, I'd get out the needle and thread of thoughtful assimilation and stitch it into my pastoral quilt. I am indeed a man of the cloth.

Sewn fabric is not anything like forged metal. Peterson, in *Five Smooth Stones*, offered me the tough material of a totally different pastoral vision. "I want a biblical base for the whole of pastoral ministry, and not just its preaching and teaching."[2] To my joyful surprise, Peterson's vision was profoundly biblical, not the latest polling-data sociological; intriguingly pastoral, not pop psychological. Peterson introduced me to ancient personalities in the mountains and villages of biblical territories who have a direct bearing on what it means to pastor, while ignoring the popular, contemporary "superstars" on the American local church stage whom we idolize (or criticize) regarding pastoral work. Peterson actually offered a non-Pauline shaped theology of pastoral work.

Again, let me emphasize that I'm all for polls and I like and have been influenced by many of the popular, well-known pastors. I like to read their books and hear them speak. I am simply insisting that these are insufficient resources for creating a personally compelling and enduring pastoral vocation.

Through the years of my formal training, I had courses in church polity, in the theology and practice of baptism and the Lord's Table, in multiple elder and congregational rule, in consensus and majority rule management, in the measure of a man and the measure of a church, in conducting weddings and presiding at funerals. I am embarrassed to admit this, but I remember one seminary course on practical pastoral ministry in which one of our textbooks was Dale Carnegie's *How To Win Friends and Influence People*. My instructor was a well-intentioned man, I'm sure, but what does a book like that say to a class of budding young pastors? Having read Peterson's discussion of the book of Ruth in *Five Smooth Stones*, I regret having ever opened Carnegie's book for advice on *being an authentic pastor*. I'm not saying Carnegie's book is of no value. It is simply a very poor substitute for the Scriptures in training pastors in significant relationship building.

With a little trepidation, I confess that even something about Eugene Peterson's book unsettles me. Peterson is known these days as the pastor's pastor. While in person he is a warm, gracious man, when it comes to formulating a biblical view of pastor, he is relentlessly firm. So, if I am bothered, it is still with a sense of deep respect for a man of his caliber. Peterson triggered my uneasiness himself in his kind words to me when he signed my copy of his book at the 1987 writers' workshop in Ann Arbor, Michigan.

For some time I have been reflecting on what Peterson wrote. "For John, sharing the life of Christ in the work of pastor. . . ." One day the phrase hit me with vision-expanding, vocation-defining impact. Those words—"sharing *the life of Christ* in the work of pastor"—compelled me to move from Peterson's profound consideration of the Old Testament Megilloth to a renewed consideration of the Messiah, Jesus Christ, as a worthy focus for envisioning the pastoral task. Not for one moment do I suggest that Eugene Peterson has neglected Jesus Christ (or Paul) as significant in shaping a pastoral vision. Jesus Christ, his life and ministry, and the apostle Paul's life and ministry simply are not the focus of *Five Smooth Stones*.

Derek Tidball comments in his book *Skillful Shepherds: An Introduction to Pastoral Theology*: "The Gospels are not just historical, theological and evangelistic documents; they are pastoral as well. Behind them lie the needs of the churches. . . . What is important is that each *pastoral need* was related back to the original gospel. . . . The needs of the

church could only be met through a deep understanding of their Lord"
(italics mine).[3]

LOOKING UP AND OUT

When I call a pastor to consider Jesus Christ as the Senior Pastor
of his church, my intention is to spotlight him as the supreme model
of pastoral work, and in this I do not want to be misunderstood. I am
not saying that pastors who hold the title "senior pastor" in their
churches are usurping a title that belongs only to Christ. Local church
"senior pastors" are *under*shepherds, nonetheless, and most acknowledge their submission to Christ.

By confessing Jesus as the Senior Pastor, I am urging all pastors—
the competent and the stumbling, the famed and the obscure, the seasoned and the novice, those
with megachurches and those
meeting in living rooms, the
seniors and the associates, the
Pentecostals and charismatics,
the evangelical cessationists and
noncessationists—to look up
and out from themselves to Jesus
Christ. Nothing is more freeing
and invigorating than looking
away from ourselves to the one
who called himself "the good
shepherd."

*Nothing is more free-
ing and invigorating
than looking away
from ourselves to the
one who called
himself "the
good shepherd."*

Imagine that America's evangelical pastors select a person they all
might proclaim as the greatest pastor on the contemporary local
church landscape. For the sake of this point, let's imagine that they
agree on one who magnetically attracts our attention and effectively
models what pastoring is all about. Here is the crucial point: that
choice pastor, if he or she is authentic, will fade gladly into the shadows cast by the blazing light of Jesus Christ, the ultimate Pastor. In
the brilliance of his glory, like the first disciples, we will all long to
hear the voice from heaven saying, "This is my Son, whom I love. *Listen to him!* " (Mark 9:7, italics mine).

We must get into the habit of gazing upon and learning from our
Lord Jesus Christ, that *great* Shepherd of his redeemed people. Paul

declares a cautionary principle that contemporary pastors must heed, "When they measure themselves by themselves and compare themselves with themselves, they are not wise" (2 Cor. 10:12). Wise pastors relentlessly fix their eyes on Jesus. From our sustained focus on Christ, we find the ability to assign ourselves to the proper place in the eyes of God, our congregations, and one another. From this proper estimate of ourselves, we will begin to develop a loving appreciation for one another even in the face of our doctrinal and denominational differences. We have much more in common by being "in Christ" than we have differences doctrinally and denominationally.

I respect the wide range of doctrinal and denominational differences as long as those differences do not form a wedge between genuinely born-again pastors. Pastors can get far beyond their reputation for comparing, envying, criticizing, or religiously competing with one another. Several years ago a staff member of our church told me about a church softball league he wanted to start. He called other pastors about the idea, adding that a church league might foster more of a sense of community among the various churches and less competition. One pastor responded sharply, "Less competition? That's what it's all about for us."

Oh, no, it isn't.

A vital question for creating and deploying an army of Spirit-empowered pastors for the generation entering the new millennium is, What was the origin of Jesus' pastoral vision?

EDUCATION IN ITS PLACE

Unlike most of us, Jesus Christ did not launch into his pastoral ministry by getting the equivalent of a seminary education. His view of pastoring was not shaped by the academic centers of his day. Everett Harrison remarks in *A Short Life of Christ*, "Of formal education, the chances are that Jesus had little. Although popularly known as a religious teacher or rabbi, his reputation was not due to technical training."[4] In fact, the glaring absence of academic credentials from Jesus' pastoral resume provoked a harsh, mocking criticism from the religious leaders toward his life and message.

The Pharisees in biting sarcasm countered the healed blind man's admiration for Christ by saying, "We know that God spoke to Moses, but as for this fellow [Jesus], we don't even know where he comes from" (John 9:29). They were verbally throwing acid in Jesus' face by saying that he was without recognized and accepted credentials. To these professionally trained religious leaders standing face to face with an undeniable miracle of mercy performed by Jesus, Jesus was still "a nobody."

The Pharisees believed that education made a rabbi "a somebody," respected and accepted. Like us, they held that training gave a person a recognized platform from which to influence others. Have we—pastors, Christian leaders, the teaching profession, and churches—fallen today into this dangerously faulty pharisaic thinking?

Education has its strategic place, but I believe it is not the place many of us think it has. Why is our belief in and dependence on a good accredited education an issue blatantly ignored by Jesus, our Chief Shepherd? Do "smarts" ever replace "heart"? Was Jesus modeling a truth for us that there is a source more profoundly forceful in shaping a pastoral vision than theological training?

Derek Tidball, in *Skillful Shepherds*, identifies a potential deficiency to pastoral ministry caused by our pursuit and possession of even the best theological education.

> *Because most pastors are taught within an academic theological context, many have been blinded to the pastoral strategies and pastoral value of the New Testament. In the ministry they have faced a different set of problems from those faced in the theological college and so dispensed with the theory they were taught as irrelevant. Having been taught no better, they have failed to appreciate the pastoral value of much doctrine and have not seen that the pastoral strategies within the New Testament could enrich their own ministries. Pastoral ministry, therefore, has often been divorced from its theological anchor and it has been poorer for it.[5]*

Pastors have to ask themselves: "What is the enduring and compelling basis for all that I do as pastor? Has my good theological education, in fact, given me a firm foundation of revealed truth for shaping my *pastoral* vision? Have I honestly asked, 'Could it be that my fine theological education actually hinders, rather than helps me *pastor?*'"

While education is good, it is not the primary platform for pastoral work. It wasn't for Jesus. Moreover, after Jesus' ascension and the arrival of the Holy Spirit on Pentecost, the early church leaders also felt the acid sting of rejection by the religiously trained elite. Their rejection was grounded in part in their being *"unschooled*, ordinary men" (Acts 4:13, italics mine). What, then, were the disciples' "pastoral" credentials? Luke records that the religious elite could not fail to notice that the disciples had been with Jesus. Their pastoral vision and stunning courage flowed from their relationship with Jesus.

Am I demeaning an academic education? Of course not. I have already confessed my deep gratitude for my own education in some fine schools. I am admitting, however, that academic training is not the source of or even the basis for pastoral vision. It was not for Jesus, nor for his earliest and very influential followers.

Before I discuss a few liabilities attendant to a theological education, I want to express four benefits of being academically trained. I do this because I am committed to the vision of thoroughly training others in the theological disciplines.

1. A respect for revealed truth. I came away from my years of formal training awed by the compelling power of the Bible to challenge some of the best minds in history, for example, Jonathan Edwards, C. S. Lewis, and Dorothy Sayers. No one can be exposed to the field of biblical and theological studies without coming away with a profound respect for revealed truth.

2. An appreciation for church history. Getting a sweep of the way God has worked in the world is a tremendous asset. Every generation needs to know its "roots." The subject of church history is staggering in terms of the mass of information available, but just one concise example—how we got the English Bible— illustrates the powerful impact of history. No earnest believer can study this small slice of church history without being deeply moved by the sacrifice men and women of faith made so that we (the English-speaking church) could have a Bible in our language.

3. The discipline of personal study. Being lazy by nature, most of us need some forced accountability and orderly structure to achieve our potential. A good theological education requires mountains of study, reflection, and dedicated learning. I thank God often not only for the content of what I learned, but for the disciplines of study necessary to learn. This is a tremendous benefit to academic training.

4. An exposure to godly men and women. I remember a conversation some fellow students and I had with a professor our first year in seminary. We were asking for advice on how to pick a major. The professor said, "Get to know the teachers and major in a man, not in a subject." (Our seminary did not have female professors at the time.) His advice was wise. Exposure to competent scholars who were also godly men made a deep and lasting impression on me. When biblical truth flows from Christlike teachers, lives are profoundly shaped for ministry.

Having offered these wonderful benefits (and there are many more), I now admit that I too have experienced the twin liabilities of an excellent theological education: pride and distancing. The spirit of pride emerges when a person revels in the biblical knowledge learned and exegetical skills acquired, as if these things make one competent to minister. As valuable as knowledge and skills are (and they are valuable), severed from an authentic daily walk with God, they may usurp their authority and begin to be viewed as the basis of ministry rather than as tools for ministry. When "tools" and "skills" usurp matters of the heart, an idolatrous attitude poisons ministry.

When "tools" and "skills" usurp matters of the heart, an idolatrous attitude poisons ministry.

Pride sets in and with it distancing. We begin to think that our education has lifted us above "the unlearned." This poisonous spirit of being distanced from uneducated people permeated the Pharisees (John 7:49). Near the end of my training at Moody Bible Institute, my mother gave me a book of poetry. Inside she wrote the following poem, which I don't think is original with her:

TO JOHN—JUNE 14, 1968

I sought to hear the voice of God
And climbed the topmost steeple;
And God declared, "Go down again;
I dwell among the people."

My mother may have sensed the danger attendant to a "good education" and gently tried to head off at the pass the ambush of pride.

Jesus, brilliant man that he was, never allowed his knowledge and skills to create distance between him and unlearned people. He was

Simply put, pastoring is bringing God to people.

wisdom incarnate who "moved into the neighborhood" (John 1:14 THE MESSAGE). He came close to us. True pastoral knowledge and skills break the distance barrier and get us close to people. The apostle Paul, excellently trained and highly gifted as he was, never used his knowledge and skills to distance himself. In fact, he did the opposite. He used the most intimate relational images to describe his ministry—the images of a nursing mother and a caring father (1 Thess. 2:7, 11).[6]

BRINGING GOD TO PEOPLE

Before we pursue the origin of pastoral identity both in Jesus and in us, let us define "pastoring." Simply put, pastoring is *bringing God to people*.[7] A pastor is one who brings God to people by imparting the Word of God (formally and informally) out of the reality of his or her life, which is undergoing authentic and continuous Christlike transformation. Just as in Jesus, the Word must become flesh in the pastor so that the transmission of truth is both exegetically sound and experientially real. This pastoral privilege and challenge—bringing God to people—is a vital incarnational aspect of Christlikeness that is expanded upon in the rest of this book.

We often hear that in the fulfillment of spiritual responsibilities, "being" precedes "doing." This is certainly true of the pastoral vision. Being, or identity, comes before doing, or ministry. From where does a man or woman receive his or her pastoral identity?

JESUS AND PROMISE

THE ORIGIN OF PASTORAL IDENTITY

STANDING on the sidewalk in front of the first church I attended as a new believer in Zion, Illinois, I was being congratulated on my first sermon preached in my hometown. Thankfully, unlike Jesus, who was rejected by his "home church" in Nazareth, I was received and affirmed by those who had watched me grow through my teen years. I was home on break from my first year of studies at Moody Bible Institute.

On the front sidewalk, a good friend of mine, Rodney Myrum, who had been a youth sponsor during my junior high and high school years at the church, put his arm on my shoulder. He looked me in the eye and said, "John, that was a good sermon. Many people are going to be influenced by you, young man, in the years to come. Mark my words, God is going to use you."

I can still feel his touch on my shoulder, hear the power of his words, and see the intensity and joy in his eyes. Rodney painted a verbal picture of my future that gripped me deeply. It was pretty heady stuff to hear as a young man. Yet the Holy Spirit used my friend's affirmation to voice a promise that lifted my vision higher, to the unfolding work of God in my life. As a novice I believed what he said. Rodney brought God to me with his kind affirmation. We live best by promises, not by prescriptions or principles.

The pastoral vision consists not only of biblically defined tasks—preaching, teaching, leading, praying, and counseling. These and other tasks are the "doing." Pastoral vision also consists of receiving our biblically defined identity. This is the "being." Education in itself does not provide for nor shape the essential call of being a "pastor." Since Jesus did not base his pastoral identity on an academic education as many of us mistakenly have done, then what was his source?

Jesus, the Nazareth carpenter, did not just by magic one day—poof!—become a pastor. Jesus' life and ministry as Chief Shepherd grew out of promise, the *rich soil of biblical revelation*. Jesus received and reflected promises and predictions from the Old Testament made about his life and mission. By his daily dependence on God the Father, these promises burst into reality. Jesus' relationship to the Father was absolutely determinative to his ministry. Relational dynamics are much more foundational for pastoral effectiveness than are educational factors. Pastoring is primarily about God and then people, not about seminary classes and earned degrees.

Most of us were trained to discover how the ancient biblical historians, prophets, and poets, under divine guidance, shaped into startling promises the hope of the Coming One, the Christ—the one who, awesome in character and life-giving in ministry, would come and dispense a mind-staggering salvation that ultimately would result in the renewal of the cosmos. "I am making everything new!" (Rev. 21:5).

> *Pastoring is primarily about God and then people, not about seminary classes and earned degrees.*

The Anointed One, God's chosen, is held in anticipated wonder, and as revelation unfolds, detail after detail about him builds, creating heart-gripping expectancy. This expectancy is captured in the cherished Christmas hymn "O Come, O Come, Emmanuel."

Immanuel did come—and died. The numbing disillusionment of the dashing of Immanuel expectancy is felt and voiced by the two disciples on the road to Emmaus when they say to the unrecognized resurrected Christ, ". . . but *we had hoped* that he was the one who was going to redeem Israel" (Luke 24:21, italics mine). They had sensed the power of promise in Jesus Christ, and with his death they concluded that the Immanuel promise was now buried with Jesus in a borrowed tomb.

A little later that evening, at supper with the stranger, the faith of the two despairing disciples was miraculously restored as Jesus—alive from the dead—was revealed when he broke the bread (Luke 24:30–31). The inquisitive stranger was none other than Jesus himself! Hope, reborn and vibrant in their hearts, propelled the two to race to Jerusalem with the incredible news of the risen Christ. Theirs was not mere intellectual assent to the pivotal salvation-history event, but an authentic, personal encounter with the resurrected Jesus Christ.

"A SOVEREIGN INDIFFERENCE"

Promises move the world. In the fullness of time, a tax-hungry Roman emperor named Augustus Caesar; an evil half-breed Judean king named Herod; an obscure and socially stigmatized Jewish couple named Joseph and Mary; and a little town with a big history called Bethlehem all found their place in making that unique window through which the Creator promised to climb, entering in human form the very world he had created. "The Word became flesh" (John 1:14).

At the arrival of the Savior of the world and Good Shepherd of God's flock, many detailed scriptural promises came to fruition. A helpless baby boy born in a stable filled with the smell of barnyard animals was the Holy One of Israel. Ancient predictions unfolded into incarnate reality as Jesus the Christ arrived. We must not forget that all these people and events entered into the story of salvation, marching into history to the steady, deep cadence of biblical promise. "It is written. . . ."

The boy grew to a man—a deeply compassionate and effectively pastoral man. Jesus did not emerge as an effective pastor by attending the Sadduccean seminars on winning people to the latest fund-raising technique or by signing up for the pharisaic workshops on trends in synagogue growth and the Roman conferences on empire builders, boomers, and busters. Jesus seemed to ignore all that we are obsessed with these days. Helmut Thielicke, commenting on Jesus' penchant for associating with ordinary people and making them the focus of his ministry, writes:

> *He appears not to be bothered at all by the fact that these are not strategi-cally important people, that they have no prominence, that they are not key figures, but only the unfortunate, lost children of the Father in heaven. He seems to ignore with a sovereign indifference the great so-called "world-historical perspectives" of his mission when it comes to one insignificant, blind, and smelly beggar, this Mr. Nobody, who is nevertheless so dear to the heart of God and must be saved.*[1]

"Ignore with a sovereign indifference"—what a great phrase and necessary aspect of pastoral ministry that needs to be recovered today. If we pay attention to what Jesus did, we will discover the source from which he developed his ironclad sense of pastoral identity and his unswerving sense of pastoral mission. That source is biblical promise activated by daily dependence on his Father.

Do you remember that dramatic, murderous moment early in Jesus' public ministry when Nazareth's admiration mutated into bloodthirsty rejection? Angry synagogue attendees attempted to push the newly announced Christ, known to them as Joseph's son, over a steep embankment. At a later time this Good Shepherd would say, "I lay down my life. . . . No one takes it from me" (John 10:17–18). But when facing death early on in Nazareth, he simply walked through the insulted mob of former neighbors who sought to be his executioners (see Luke 4:14–30).

What in the world had Jesus done to provoke such a violent response? He had simply declared that he was biblical promise incar-nate. He had defined his identity and mission as the fulfillment of Isaiah's promise of the Spirit-anointed one coming to bring salvation. Jesus, in Nazareth's synagogue, had unrolled the scroll of Isaiah and read these words, "The Spirit of the Lord is on me. . . ." *Promise had become person. The Word had become flesh.* At Jesus' baptism by John and after his blistering confrontation with Satan in the wilderness, he became Spirit-empowered: "Jesus returned to Galilee *in the power of the Spirit* " (Luke 4:14, italics mine).

We know that Jesus grew up in Nazareth and received training along with his peers. But Jesus exceeded them even to the point that as a twelve-year-old he amazed the scholars who held session in the temple courts. Jesus, like any other Jewish son, received the customary education, and he grew in wisdom (see Luke 2:46–52).

Again, we must ask: Where exactly did Jesus ground his identity and mission? Where did he resource his pastoral vision? Not in the accumulation of academic wisdom, good as it was, but in revelation promise (the Scriptures) and appropriated power (the Spirit).

R. T. France writes: "In the Jewish world of the first century A.D. Jesus of Nazareth was a man apart. This is seen not least in his use of the Old Testament. . . . The essence of his new application was that he saw the fulfillment of the predictions and foreshadowings of the Old Testament in himself and his work."[2] The Old Testament, the inscripturated revelation promise of God, provided the central source of Jesus' growing sense of identity and his predicted mission.

"THE BOOK FOR ME"

We cannot overlook these fundamental issues about Jesus. The way Jesus grew into his vocational identity has a direct bearing on how men and women will define and enter into their identities as pastors. Christopher J. H. Wright drives home the point that Jesus grounded his identity in biblical revelation. "It was the Old Testament which helped Jesus understand Jesus. Who did he think he was? What did he think he was to do? The answers came from his Bible, the Hebrew scriptures. . . . His Hebrew Bible provided the shape of his own identity."[3]

No more urgent quest can be undertaken by pastors than to ground their identity where Jesus grounded his. Beneath a good theological education, beneath good communication skills, beneath all that goes into being an effective pastor, there must be an identity grounded on the eternal bedrock of biblical promise. "The B-I-B-L-E—yes, that's the book for me. . . ."

Douglas Webster, in his book *A Passion for Christ*, raises this question: "If Jesus' experience of God is guided and inspired by the content of Scripture, should not those who follow Jesus and *seek to become like him* discipline themselves through the power of the Spirit of God to be molded mentally, emotionally, and spiritually by the Word of God?" (italics mine).[4] Do pastors believe that in the daily, sometimes tedious expression of their calling, they are working to the enduring, steady cadence of revelation promise? Do they find confidence in God the Father, who sees pastors (undershepherds) through the same loving eyes that watched his Son, the Chief Shepherd? Didn't Jesus say to his first undershepherds, "Peace be with you! As the Father has sent me, I am sending you" (John 20:21)? The key word is "as." The Father stands ready to impart through promise and to activate through power pastoral ministry in today's shepherds just as he did for Jesus, the Chief Shepherd.

All the Father asks of us today is what he received from Jesus. Jesus offered daily waiting upon and obedience to God the Father as the source of personal identity and pastoral ministry. Identity flows from intimacy. Do pastors find energy and encouragement in the truth that the promises that shaped Jesus' pastoral identity and mission also shape theirs? Pastors live "in Christ," in the Anointed One. We are called undershepherds, apprentices to the Master Shepherd. As we consider the life of Jesus in combination with the purpose of the Father that we be "conformed to the likeness of his Son" (Rom. 8:29), we realize that we are to be like Jesus in character and power, in identity and mission.

> The Father stands ready to impart through promise and to activate through power pastoral ministry in today's shepherds just as he did for Jesus, the Chief Shepherd.

As shepherds we are apprenticed to the Chief Shepherd and are invited to live with the same empowerment that Jesus had. Only in one act is Jesus the Christ completely and uniquely set apart from us. He was (and is) spotlessly pure, sinless, and as such, he died a unique substitutionary death in payment for sin. No other person or pastor can ever duplicate that. Calvary's cross is his alone.

CALLED BY NAME

Promise is the ancient written Word of God becoming the present, living voice of God—a voice that calls out our deepest identity and equips us for our predestined mission. Jeremiah, on the brink of his tough ministry, received from the Lord, "Before I formed you in the womb I knew you, before you were born I set you apart" (Jer. 1:5).

God knew Jeremiah by name, and Jesus, as Good Shepherd, knows each of his sheep by name. It certainly stands to reason then that Jesus knows and calls his undershepherds by name. This is a vital truth riveting biblical promise to the individual pastor. "The personal name is the most important part of speech in our language. . . . The act of naming . . . has enormous significance."[5]

Pastor, on the brink of or neck-deep in your ministry, do you live in the confidence that God knows you, calls you by name, and is with you? Do you find strength in the truth that he knows *the deep you* with whom you are perhaps out of touch or of whom you are unaware? Do you depend on and find courage in the truth that Jesus is also called "Immanuel"? God is with you! One of the primary promises giving life and courage to the pastoral task is this promise of the divine presence. "I am with you always, to the very end of the age" (Matt. 28:20).

Deepest identity is the "you" God has created you to be. We must become the person God had in mind when he willed to create us. This God-defined identity may escape us because we do not even know it ourselves. Our deepest identity may lie buried under the accumulated wreckage of sin, our own sins and those of others. Nothing or no one can call it forth, integrated and invigorated for life, but God alone.

We do not and cannot acquire deep identity from biological parents or biblical professors. It is not a social role or a vocational choice. Deep, authentic identity is created, called out, and shaped by the living God. The vine and branches metaphor used by Jesus was not intended to become a Christian wall hanging or to spawn cheap Christianized art. Only in the intimacy of abiding do we discover identity and ministry. It's true: apart from Jesus we can do nothing (John 15:5).

> We experience promise as activated pastoral ministry as we imitate Jesus — that is, as we wait on, listen to, and obey the Father.

Promise ("I know you. I will be with you") is an active, divine word meeting us in the chaos of the present moment and propelling us with strategic, ordered, and empowered purpose into the next moment, the next hour, day, week, lifetime. Promise is a spoken magnetic force just ahead of us, pulling

and shaping the strong metal of our God-created and called-out identity. We are empowered to enter into God's expressed purpose for our
lives as a well-defined person. We experience promise as activated
pastoral ministry as we imitate Jesus—that is, as we wait on, listen to,
and obey the Father.

C. S. Lewis describes the coming into being of our truest identity
as God's creation when he describes Jane's remarkable and surprising
conversion in the third book of his space trilogy. In *That Hideous
Strength*, we are introduced to Jane, who is met by the personal Presence (God), and in that meeting everything changes for her. She is
changed in a moment of time, Lewis writes, "too short to be called
time at all." In this unexpected encounter, Jane begins to perceive and
understand her new, God-designed identity.

> *In this height and depth and breadth the little idea of herself which she had
> hitherto called* me *dropped down and vanished. . . . The name* me *was the
> name of a being whose existence she had never suspected, a being that did
> not yet fully exist but which was being demanded. It was a person (not the
> person she had thought), yet also a thing, a thing made, made to please
> Another and in Him to please all others, a thing being made at this very
> moment, without its choice, in a shape it never dreamed of.*[6]

In God's inexorable presence the little idea called "me" dies and
God's idea of "me" comes into being. It is an identity from God and
for God. This personal entering into our God-designed "self" must
be the experience of pastors (and all Christ-followers). Only as *we*
experience profound change will we ever hope to see life transformation in the people in our charge.

Maybe my story can help illustrate what I am coming to understand about the emergence of personal identity, whether we are pastors or not. Our vocation is secondary to our identity. In telling my
story I am not saying that all pastors have to experience an existential
crisis like I have had in order to be good pastors. I have heard of many
other less dramatic experiences that God has used to call out the deep
identity of his sons and daughters. I simply want to illustrate the
importance of an emerging *God-given identity*.

For years I ran from my past. My father was an alcoholic, a com-
pulsive gambler, and an immoral, angry man. Yet he cultivated a "nice
guy" persona. My parents' divorce left me the victim of a broken home

at age ten. Not until my early forties did I get in touch with the truth that the divorce had also left me internally devastated as a boy. My soul was ransacked. I was from a broken home, and I had a broken heart. The wound was so profoundly painful that I poured as much psychological concrete (technically called "denial") as I could over the gaping holes in my soul caused by the abandonment of my dad. Yet, with all his personal deficiencies, he remained for me, as any dad remains to his son, a very significant person. He was my father.

My father had been a career navy officer and an accomplished photographer, but his greatest photographic effect was on me. His many sinful choices left on the sensitive film of my soul many images of despair: feelings of abandonment, rage, and inferiority. Men without dads feel sidelined, kept from getting to "suit up" for the game called life. I made it my quest to please people so I could stay happy and to pursue significance through acquisition of knowledge, training, and the ability to communicate and entertain. I too was loved and affirmed as a "nice guy" and as a somewhat proficient pastor. Then for me, as for Jane in C. S. Lewis's story, "the change came."

STRUGGLING FOR IDENTITY

None of us can ever run fast enough to escape our past. It will catch up. During my early forties I began to think, with hellish horror, that I was fulfilling the old proverb "Like father, like son." Perhaps you can sense something of the horror, the hell I felt I faced. I had spent years building an identity that was the polar opposite of my father's. As a good hero in the alcoholic home, I set out to redeem the family name. Yet, in my forties I found that my father's identity was profoundly "in me" fighting to get out. I was terrified. He had permeated my soul. "The sins of the fathers visited."

When I began to feel strong and wild impulses that, if acted upon, could bring dishonor to Christ, destroy my marriage and my four precious daughters, shame my church, and sideline me from ministry, I was rocked with fear. In torturous agony I kept asking, "Where are these destructive, sinister impulses coming from? Nice guys, especially pastors, aren't suppose to feel like this, are they?"

At a leadership conference at Willow Creek Community Church, I heard Bill Hybels confess something of the horror he found in the darkness of his own soul. Because Bill is often asked to sit in on disciplinary sessions for fallen Christian leaders, he has heard stories of how pastors struggled and then crashed their lives into the ditch of addiction or immorality.

Hybels admitted that the struggles of those he heard who had fallen were, to his dismay, his struggles too. So he decided to do the smart thing, the humbling thing. He sought and received professional help. When I heard him make this frank confession, some inner shame barrier in me was broken, and I gave myself permission to get help for my struggles as well. And I did.

In our city there is a ministry devoted to helping pastors and church leaders with personal or vocational struggles. A wise, older, and godly counselor, with skillful and gentle questioning, led me back down the lanes of my past, interpreting many tragic events for me— something no one had ever done for me. My wild impulses were discovered to be eruptions of suppressed rage. Rage is not necessarily *out*-rage.

Inner rage stems from traumatic events that receive no meaningful explanation. For example, the way I learned about the divorce that split my parents apart was from my mother, who called me on a hot Tennessee summer night and said, "Johnny, you have a new daddy." I remember the shock to my soul and how I thought, *New daddy? What happened to the old one?* No one walked me through the divorce in terms a ten-year-old could understand.

Under my counselor's wise direction, I became unfrozen emotionally and started growing into inner adulthood. I discovered that I was truly free from crafting an identity solely based on escaping my past. I plunged into discovering how my past *in God's hands* was scripted to contribute to his identity of me. I could look back on vast junkyards of inner wreckage and recognize that *for me* it is also incredibly true that "in all things God works for the good of those who love him, who have been called according to his purpose" (Rom. 8:28). I could, without crippling shame, embrace all my past, no longer with searing feelings of inferiority, but with acceptance. It was an acceptance wet with grief, but acceptance nonetheless.

Pastorally I had to personally grapple with the *wisdom* of God in planning my past. To use Eugene Peterson's metaphor, I had to become "God's spy searching out the ways of grace" written into the pages of my life.[7] Even the more tragic paragraphs of particular pages were part of God's sweeping story of glorious salvation.

More than in anything or anyone else, I now am grounding my identity in promise. God's promise that he chose me before the foundation of the world to be his and to be an undershepherd of God's flock brings ballast in the sometimes turbulent waters of ministry. I believe with a deep sense of joy that *"all the days ordained for me were written in [God's] book before one of them came to be"* (Ps. 139:16, italics mine). I am finding myself to be a character in God's continuing story of grace.

Not all that happened to me or all that I've done can in itself be called good. Some of it is rightly called evil. But I believe, and pastors proclaim, that salvation is the conquering of evil—personal, social, and cosmic—through Christ. We have an author of salvation who is able to write evil's worst lines into an ultimately breathtaking story of awesome grace! A quick reflection on the lives of Joseph and Jesus, David and Paul, is all that is required to establish this remarkable truth.

> *We have an author of salvation who is able to write evil's worst lines into an ultimately breathtaking story of awesome grace!*

Pastors do not find a compelling sense of identity in education, in personality, nor in a "self-made image" constructed out of what is the best while denying what is the most frightful about their pasts. At some point we must yield to what A. W. Tozer wrote concerning God's wisdom as it applies to our lives. "Wisdom, among other things, is the ability to devise perfect ends and to achieve those ends by the most perfect means. . . . Not only could His acts not be better done: a better way to do them could not be imagined."[8] Tozer is not saying that everything that happens to us is "good." He is saying that everything about us is within the boundary of God's comprehensive wisdom.

As I reflected on the disjunction in my own history between what was painfully tragic and, at points, very real evil, and my dawning awareness of the comprehensive wisdom of God, I crashed into the brick wall of decision. The hard choice that I had to make centered on nothing short of total surrender to the goodness of God *in the par-*

ticulars of my life. Larry Crabb captures for us the agony and the glory of that surrender.

> *No one will conclude that God is good by studying life. The evidence powerfully suggests otherwise. Belief in God's goodness and the worship that naturally flows from this confidence depends on the revealing work of the Holy Spirit. When he ushers us into the presence of ultimate goodness, when our darkest tragedy is pierced by one glimpse of invisible glory, then faith is born.*[9]

I was leading up to the point where I crashed into the wall of decision. I had to have it out with God over the specific, ugly details in the history of my life. One day in my study, while in worship, reflecting on God's wisdom, I asked him, "How can you be wise in not letting me have my father for thirty years? What is so almighty wise about that? It has left me wounded, wildly impulsive, and feeling deeply inferior. Wise, eh? If this is wisdom, who needs it? Other men have their dads; why couldn't I have had mine? It has left a gaping hole, a Grand Canyon in my soul!"

The Lord God answered, not audibly, but truly to me, "Why do you think I allowed that deep and massive hole to be painfully and shamefully carved into your soul?"

"That *is* the question. How is not having my dad all that wise?" I answered.

God softly and firmly answered, and his answer humbled me, literally doubled me over to the floor. "John, you have that Grand Canyon in your soul so that I, your heavenly Father, can fill it."

RECEIVING SHALOM

If my past had rocked me, God's answer shocked me. I was momentarily shattered. Then God began rearranging my interior self. Someone has said, "When Jesus came, he blew everything to pieces, and when I saw where the pieces fell, I knew I was free."

In conversation with God, I was being introduced personally and profoundly and deeply to *shalom*, to the wholeness, to the reintegration of a life shattered by abandonment and disintegrated by sin. God was bringing me salvation through his appointed agent, the one who heals the brokenhearted. As Larry Crabb describes it, I needed and received a "revealing work of the Holy Spirit."

God's shocking yet inspiring answer caused me to laugh, to cry, to exalt in God. Worship flowed like rushing waters. I found myself saying, "Oh, that other men could have a canyon so big in their souls so that you, O Lord, could fill it for them! Too bad other guys haven't been abandoned by their fathers." Isn't that wildly hilarious? I was having compassion for men from *non*broken homes.

In the thrill of God's "interpretation" of my past, I discovered an identity and a reason for my personal existence. All that I had received and interpreted as shameful and wounding, God had wisely given as his means to shape my reason for being. In this encounter with God, my purpose in life became clear: *I exist so that others can experience God as Father.* Not just that others can know *about* God as Father, but that they can enter into the wonder of meaningful, conversational life with God as Father. All that I had been through, good and bad, happened as I was on the divine Potter's wheel. I was (and am) being shaped in such a way, sometimes painfully, so that my soul can be filled with God. Amazing!

Everything falls into place—personal history, education, giftedness, personality temperament and abilities, acquired training and competencies—only after our identity as designed by God is called out in our personal encounter with him. Until then we play at existence, dabble at pastoring, and hydroplane over deep purpose and meaning. We miss what it means to be holy in the way Jesus was holy.

> *Everything falls into place ... only after our identity as designed by God is called out in our personal encounter with him.*

A common and popular error is to link "being holy" with our good (Christian) behaviors. To correct this deadly error we must see the marvelous and liberating truth that our identity is the wellspring of authentic, Christlike holiness. In his book *Threshold of the Future,* Michael Riddell calls believers back to the vibrant, fearless, and joyful holiness exhibited in Jesus' life and relationships. Riddell establishes the fact that holiness is primarily separation to God in which our identity is called out; holiness is not contained in the fear-producing idea of separation from the "world."

*A Christian understanding of holiness will mean freedom from fear. . . .
The good news in Christ is that fearfulness has come to an end. . . . The
secret of this freedom from fear lies in a strong sense of our identity in
Christ. . . .*

*Here is the central truth of Christian holiness: it consists not in behav-
ior, but in identity. Identity of course will influence behavior. . . . When we
know we are safe in Christ, we are free to go wherever we want and mix
with whoever we want, and do it without fear.*[10]

Jesus periodically heard his Father say, "You are my Son, whom I
love; with you I am well pleased" (Luke 3:22; cf. Matt. 3:17; 17:5;
Mark 1:11; Luke 9:35; John 12:28). Every pastor must hear the Father's
voice saying the exact same thing to him or her. I have. Sometimes
the Spirit has born witness directly to my spirit that I am God's child.
At other times God has affirmed me as his son through the ministry
of others. I am exploring and enjoying the truth that my identity is
grounded in God and his phenomenal promises to me.

We must quiet ourselves regularly in solitude and allow the bonding we have with God to embrace us and the Spirit to cry out in us,
"Abba, Father!" People may seduce us into being with them too much,
to our detriment and theirs. We must pull away in solitude and silence
so that we can contemplate Christ, who is the ultimate promise of
God. In this intimacy we revel in that we are in him and he is in us.

One of the reasons Jesus practiced solitude was so that his identity
as the Promised One could be called out by the Father. It can be no
less for us. If our Chief Shepherd grounded his identity in the revelation promise and real presence of the Father, we undershepherds must
ground our identities there as well. A pastor must substitute nothing
or no one for the Father's voice of affirmation and commission. His
voice is brought to us on the wavelength of biblical promise empowered by the Spirit as we daily depend on God. "Jesus shows us how
God intended human life to be lived. Through his capacity to love,
communicate, think, and worship, he demonstrated not only what it
means to be spiritual, but what *it means to be human*" (italics mine).[11]

We are invited to probe this mystery of promise meeting person.
We must seize the result: our real identity bursting into clarity. There
is a "both/and" formation to the emergence of pastoral identity. It was
not just my "existential encounter" with God that brought clarity to
my "being." It was that encounter *within the framework of biblical truth*

(promise) that exploded healing and hope, vision and purpose in me. Without biblical truths such as God's sovereignty, wisdom, mercy, and love, the encounter would have been emotional yet empty—and probably fleeting. On the other hand, those same truths were sterile propositions that I had received and transmitted for years until "the change came." I am not grounding my identity in an existential encounter alone, but in an encounter planned by my heavenly Father and interpreted by his eternal Word. The bedrock of pastoral identity is the Word of God made thrillingly alive by the work of the Holy Spirit.

"Sharing the life of Christ in the work of pastor." I am discovering that "sharing the life of Christ" is the work and outworking of all that it means to pastor. Grasping biblical promise to our souls, we hear God's voice saying, "Pastor my people. I call you out by name. All my ways of wisdom have been shaping the deepest and most authentic you, the being you long to be, the you that is most like my Son."

Jesus, our Chief Shepherd, sourced his pastoral identity in biblical promise that the Father called out into incarnate reality. He also sourced his pastoral mission in Spirit-empowerment, as we will see in the next chapter.

JESUS AND THE SPIRIT

THE SOURCE OF POWER
FOR THE PASTORAL TASK

TWO staff members and I were bowed in prayer over a young wife and mother in our church family. This young lady, Cathy (not her real name), was struggling with some deep and painful issues in her relationship with God. We had just finished a Wednesday night class on spiritual warfare taught by Dr. Victor Matthews, former professor of systematic theology at Grand Rapids Baptist Seminary. Cathy asked for prayer.

As the others were praying for Cathy, I asked God the Father to help me serve this lady, to help her get out of her agony into the peace that Jesus promises. Silently I prayed, "Father, I need your help here. Cathy is struggling, crying. What can you show me, O God, to help shepherd her into your arms of acceptance, forgiveness, and peace?"

Then something unusual happened—so unusual that it confused me at first. I clearly saw in my mind's eye the silhouette of the underside of a Boeing 747 flying from the bottom of my mental screen to the top. Initially I chided myself for not paying attention to the moment and questioned my compassion for this struggling person. "John, concentrate. Your mind is wandering. Get focused on this lady's agony." I still saw the distinct silhouette of the jet. It now flew from right to left across the vision of my mind's eye. What was going on?

I had the most radical, unsettling thought, a thought that my particular theological background has a very hard time accepting. "Oh no, Lord! You're not telling me something about Cathy, are you? I'm not supposed to believe you operate like this. This all went out with the first-century apostles, didn't it?"

Apparently the Father took my initial prayerful plea for pastoral guidance for Cathy more seriously than I did. So, tentatively believing that God was actually helping me with Cathy, I ventured to timidly ask this question to her, "Does a jet plane mean anything to you, Cathy?"

"No," she responded.

Oops! Now what do I do? On the one hand, I felt like saying, "See, God, I knew this was hokey," but on the other hand, I surprisingly found myself persisting with Cathy, "Have you made any decisions while on a jet plane that are significant to you?"

The dam broke. Cathy's crying turned to sobbing, her body convulsing as she cried out, "When I left the field as a missionary to come back to the States, sitting on the plane I felt I had failed God! I believed that I had deeply disappointed him and that I was settling for his second best. I have come to believe that all the friction in my marriage to Joe (not his real name) is God's punishment because I did not stay on the mission field!"

I began crying. I was crying over Cathy's pain that came gushing up from the deep inner wells of pent-up grief and guilt. Compounding her guilt was the anguish coming from the pit of hopeless agony that stemmed from her belief that her turbulent marriage would never be fully blessed by God. But I was also crying because the Spirit of God had enabled me, her pastor, in a moment of helplessness, "to see into her" and to ask the penetrating, precise question that brought her back, received and loved, into her heavenly Father's arms.

Does this happen all the time in conversation and prayer? No. Does it happen occasionally? Yes. What does this mean?

EMPOWERED BY THE SPIRIT

Pastors are equipped with the same promises and same power that Jesus, the Chief Shepherd and Supreme Pastor, had in his earthly ministry. Just as our pastoral identity is rooted in God's promise that we are his sons and daughters and Jesus' brothers and sisters, whom Jesus delights in unashamedly (Heb. 2:12), so our pastoral mission is empowered by the same Spirit who empowered Jesus for his pastoral ministry.

We make a grave theological and pastoral error if we attribute all the expressions of power in Jesus' earthly ministry *only* to his essential being as the incarnate Second Person of the Trinity. I am solidly evangelical in my commitment to the deity of Jesus Christ, but to observe his pastoral life and conclude that it is only because of his deity that he said and did what he did, is to allow no hope of Jesus ever being a real model for us. To follow him as Chief Shepherd, to experience him as Teacher to whom we are apprenticed as trainees who are to become like him, is completely futile if all he said and did was traceable only to his deity. If his ministry life rested completely on his deity, then we are all hopelessly isolated from ever living out his invitation, "Follow me."

> *Pastors are equipped with the same promises and same power that Jesus, the Chief Shepherd and Supreme Pastor, had in his earthly ministry.*

None of us will ever be the Second Person of the Trinity incarnate. We know that "to follow" means entering into that exciting discipling adventure of *becoming like Jesus*. We are to be conformed to the image of our Teacher and Pastor in both character and power. I will expand on this exciting truth of empowered transformation in chapter 7.

In Luke 4 we see Jesus basing his identity and mission on the biblical promise of Isaiah 61. What does the promise include? It includes Spirit-empowerment. "Jesus returned to Galilee in the *power of the Spirit*," and told his listeners in the synagogue, "The Spirit of the Lord is on me" (Luke 4:14, 18, italics mine). Luke's commitment to precision leads him to write, "And the *power* of the Lord was present for him to heal the sick" (Luke 5:17, italics mine). Jesus was sensitive to those times when the Holy Spirit empowered him to do supernatural things. About Luke's account of Jesus and the Spirit, Gerald Hawthorne remarks, "Clearly, then, for Luke the Holy Spirit, who is to be distinguished from Jesus, is that divine power outside of Jesus which comes down upon Jesus, which stands over him, which is at work within him and through him, which both inspires and empowers him. Jesus thus begins his mission armed with the Spirit and goes forward to accomplish that mission in the power of the Spirit."[1]

The controlling idea of Hawthorne's book is that Jesus did not do supernatural ministry on the basis of his being the Second Person of the Trinity. His ministry was done in the power of the Holy Spirit; the same Holy Spirit that pastors (and all believers) receive when they receive the salvation of God. It is the person and ministry of the Spirit that makes it practically possible for believers—the empowered church—to be like Jesus in character and power. Jesus was a Spirit-empowered human being.

The apostle Peter points us to a significant distinction. When the Spirit was poured out at Pentecost, Peter, briefly rehearsing Jesus' life and ministry, described Jesus as *"a man* accredited by God to you by miracles, wonders and signs, which *God did among you through him,* as you yourselves know" (Acts 2:22, italics mine). To Peter, a very close companion and observer of Jesus for three years, Jesus was a *God-empowered man.* Saying this does not in any way detract from the fact that Jesus is also the incarnate Word, Second Person of the Trinity. Saying Jesus was a God-empowered *man* is no threat to Jesus' deity. Jesus Christ is 100 percent God and 100 percent human being united forever in one person.

Jesus himself, in argument with the Pharisees over his deliverance ministry, declared that he was empowered by the Holy Spirit. In Matthew 12:28 Jesus does not say that he drives out demons because he is divine. No, he says that he drives out demons by the empowerment of the Spirit. "But if I drive out demons *by the Spirit of God,* then the kingdom of God has come upon you" (italics mine).

This distinction radically informs my emerging vision of pastoring. Our Chief Shepherd willingly engaged the pastoral task the way we all must. When Jesus "emptied himself" (Phil. 2:7 RSV), he leveled the playing field of pastoral ministry. He willingly entered our territory as we do, and he lived among us with the same resources with which God equips us to live and minister. He leaned heavily on revelation promise (the Scriptures) and depended daily on supernatural empowerment (the Spirit of God). As Hawthorne notes, "Jesus depended on the Spirit of God," and this "is but one additional proof of the genuineness of his humanity."[2]

All during his earthly ministry, Jesus remained surrendered to the will of the Father. We are called to the same pastoral vision, and we can do it—not as perfectly as Jesus did, but with the same Spirit-empowerment that he had.

Empowerment includes the gifts of healing (1 Cor. 12:9). This topic raises many questions, I know. Yet I believe that on a specific occasion the Spirit empowered me with a "gift of healing." I am not a healer, yet I was privileged to cooperate with Jesus in the healing of a newborn boy who, after a few hours, went into Respiratory Distress Syndrome.

I was awed at God's goodness as I read portions of the father and mother's comments about this tragic crisis in their son's first hours out of the womb.

> On Oct. 26, 1993, God blessed us with the birth of our first son . . . but in less than two hours he developed a life-threatening breathing disorder. . . . His body was unable to produce enough surfactant which keeps the lungs from collapsing after exhaling. . . . [The child was to be moved to another hospital] because he was in critical condition, and without the help of a ventilator he would probably die. . . . Before they transferred [him], they brought him into our room as if to say, "Take a last look." He was limp and lifeless. . . . At that moment disbelief overwhelmed me . . . at this point I was preparing for the worst. . . . [I]t terrified me to think we may lose him so soon. . . . I was at the most helpless point in my life.

As pastor to this young couple, I entered into this traumatic time with them. But what could I do? I felt helpless in the face of such terrible agony. I could pray. And I did. I was there to pray for the limp and almost lifeless little boy who was strapped down to his crib and hooked to an incredible array of machines. After being in the neonatal intensive care unit I journaled:

> Scrubbing my hands with surgeon's soap allowed me to see and touch the baby boy, two days old and still not breathing on his own, his blood by-passing his lungs, going to his heart deprived of oxygen. How odd to think that I was scrubbed clean so that I, along with an anxious mother and father, could take my place at the edge of helplessness and watch efficient nurses follow procedures and listen to the sounds of state-of-the-art medical machines.

The edge of helplessness is a high ledge of hope. Poised there and scrubbed and gowned, I peer into the vast unseen territory where Jesus Christ, just as busy and certainly more proficient, does his "medical rounds," needing no machines and yet not minding those he sees. He gazes upon the baby with eyes of love and marvels at the artistic beauty of his Father's hand. A new being bearing God's image, so tiny, so needy, an infant and incarnate promise to his waiting mother, whose red eyes and tentative voice signal the inescapable tension of her helplessness and hope. Jesus' presence is real, his love sensed, his power invading and superseding all other powers directed toward the healing of this little boy. He invites us over into his startling realm, and with a calculated leap of faith, we land upright and eager in his kingdom. All kingdom ministry operates powerfully from the human side at the edge of helplessness. Human helplessness is what Jesus called "poor in spirit," and those who feel its reality and accept its primacy in ministry will receive "the kingdom of God." The edge of helplessness is the ledge of hope overlooking the surprising invasion of Jesus Christ the King. Trusting Jesus means walking by faith into his territory and, not only watching him work, but experiencing the joy of working along with him.

The little boy lived. The young couple wrote, "We are still praising God for [our son's] miraculous recovery, and through this difficult time we have experienced God's grace in a very helpless situation."

> *Trusting Jesus means walking by faith into his territory and, not only watching him work, but experiencing the joy of working along with him.*

I am convinced that Jesus performed a miracle of healing power through me as I prayed. I did not heal the infant boy, but a real, present Jesus in that neonatal intensive care unit did. I was privileged to partner with Christ in a miracle. The young couple believe that their son was miraculously delivered from impending death in the early hours of his life. The Spirit distributes "gifts of healing" deliberately and sovereignly as he wills. The Spirit expressed in that moment Jesus' power to heal, and I felt the joy and wonder of being yoked to Jesus in that supernatural moment.

Does this mean that everyone our church's elders or I pray for is healed? No, but in view of the sovereignly given and compassion-driven "gifts of healing" distributed by the Spirit, we have a strong boldness and joyful freedom to ask for healing. If healing does not occur, we are confident the Father still is loving and all-wise in his dealings with people, even in suffering, pain, and death.

Through both proclaimed Word and powerful deed, the Lord Jesus Christ will be revealed in the world through the church, his body. Empowered pastors have the extraordinary privilege of leading an empowered church into the next millennium. The Spirit who anointed Jesus for his ministry as Chief Shepherd has been given to pastors and other believers. As we seek the Father for greater empow-erment by the Spirit, he will surely answer with greater outpourings to fill our lives.

Relying on and living in the power of the Spirit, pastors find that all the other resources on which they previously leaned for competent and effective min-istry find the proper place in their life. Their personal history becomes significant within God's story of grace, their edu-cation becomes a tool rather than the base of ministry, their giftedness as a communicator

> As we seek the Father for greater empowerment by the Spirit, he will surely answer with greater outpourings to fill our lives.

becomes an avenue for bringing God himself to people and not just God's truth. This is the kind of pastor I long to be and little by little am becoming.

NOT OUT ON A LIMB

What does this supernatural dimension mean to my life? It cer-tainly opens the door to the unusual. One Sunday morning during our third service, as I was worshiping with the church family during a time of singing, a graphic image of a handgun formed in my mind. I thought this was odd and tried to "shake it off." As I continued to sing, the unsettling image persisted. I was wondering what in the world was happening to me. Growing in the realization that the Spirit imparts detailed information to us, I asked in silent prayer, "Lord, what is this? Why am I seeing a handgun while I'm trying to worship?"

Within my spirit I heard the Spirit saying, "There is a very desperate person in the church, a person contemplating suicide, even to the point of handling the gun."

In dialogue with God I said, "Oh, great! What am I supposed to do? You don't want me to walk up to that pulpit and tell people this, do you?" The Spirit answered by drawing my attention to Romans 12:6: "If a man's gift is prophesying, let him use it in proportion to his faith." The Lord seemed to be asking me, "Do you have the faith to risk reporting what you are seeing and sensing in the spiritual realm?"

The entire episode happened quickly. The Spirit pressed the issue of my obedience of faith in reporting what I believed was a prophetic revelation, a word of knowledge. "Lord, I don't care what people will think, I want to be obedient to you."

I walked to the pulpit to make the transition into the message. I began by saying, "This is a little unusual for me, but the Lord was impressing me while we were worshiping that someone here is seriously contemplating suicide. I may be wrong, but I believe someone is here who has handled a gun, a handgun. If so, the Lord wants you to know that he extends hope and life to you. You do not have to take such a drastic measure."

I proceeded, then, into the rest of the service. After the service no one approached me, saying, "Pastor, it's me. I'm the desperate one." As a matter of fact, no one even mentioned anything about my prophetic word. I felt like, "Great, Lord! I knew you might do this—let me climb out on a limb and then saw myself off. I really blew it."

Nothing happened until the next day at about 2:15 P.M. when I received a phone call. "John, this is Susan. I know who was going to commit suicide." She continued, "Last night a close friend of mine came to my house in tears. She cried and cried. She was deeply depressed and said that her life isn't worth living. She can't take the pressure, and she wants to kill herself. John, because I was in the third service when you spoke about suicide, I asked my friend, 'Do you have a handgun?' She said that she did and that if she weren't in my house at the moment, she would put the bullets in it and kill herself. I went with her to her house, and I got the gun away. It is a small handgun. John, never in the world would I have asked my friend about a gun had you not said what you did. I told my friend, 'Do you know how much God loves you? Let me tell you what God revealed to John yesterday. God loves you so much to have John share that so that I can help you now.' By the way, John, my friend was in the first service. Don't ever be disobedient to what the Lord shows you."

When I shared this phone call with the church staff, one of my fellow pastors observed that the "word of knowledge" was really intended for the helping friend who needed to hear it so that she would be equipped to intervene on behalf of her desperate friend.

Are the so-called sign gifts, the more supernatural gifts, still operable to express God's immediate presence and redemptive power? Could it be, for instance, that the gift of prophecy *properly understood* is operable today? While answering these questions requires more discussion (chapter 11), I believe I was ushered into their reality in my own pastoral ministry. To enter into this dimension of empowered pastoral ministry, we must accept the call to be yoked to and to learn from Jesus.

JESUS AND HIS YOKE

THE "IMMANUEL" OF
AUTHENTIC PASTORAL MINISTRY

RESTLESS, I tossed and turned on the bed in an eighth-floor apartment in a large city in Ukraine, the first Soviet bloc country to declare independence. It was late Sunday night, and I was to start teaching classes on Monday in an evangelical mission's new Bible institute, a school designed to equip Christian leaders to minister to a city of a million inhabitants as well as to the surrounding villages.

After a long and tiring flight, I had arrived in Kiev on Saturday, but my luggage had not. One of my suitcases contained all my notes for the classes. I stayed overnight in Kiev with a friend who was also from Grand Rapids in the hope my luggage would come Sunday. It did not. Due to schedule constraints, we had to leave Kiev and get to the Bible institute, a good eleven-hour trip on a highway with potholes the size of foxholes—the military kind.

Late that night in a bleak, cold Ukrainian city, tired from the exhausting, bumpy ride from Kiev, disoriented somewhat from jet lag, and depressed about having none of my belongings, my mind raced and my spirit worried about starting the classes with no notes. All I had was my Bible, a legal pad, and whatever I could remember in my head about the course content.

As I tossed and turned on the bed in a strange room, the Lord and I got into a conversation. You can guess how it started.

"Why, Lord? Why is this happening to me? I'm over here in this dreary city to do your work. I'll have to wear the same clothes I've had on for days, underwear included. I face a full day of teaching tomorrow, teaching in a way I have never taught before—with an interpreter. And I have no notes!"

The yoke. Jesus did not desert me, though my luggage and enthusiasm had. What good would the doctrine of God's omnipresence do for me now in this situation? The yoked Lord, becoming active in this troubled conversation, asked in my spirit, "John, what was the title, again, of the course you are to teach?"

"Spiritual Nurture and Discipleship, Lord."

"What is it about?"

"It is about how you, Lord, nurture our souls. How we are replenished, nourished by you and the life you offer. You know, Lord, the promises in Matthew 11:28–30. It is about the spiritual disciplines that are available to us to enter into your gracious, accepting presence and receive from you all that you promise."

"So, you're going to tell these Ukrainian pastors and worship leaders that I, the Lord, nurture the soul?"

"Yes, Lord, I am . . . or I was, but now I'm in a bind. I have none of my materials."

"John, right now, in these depressing circumstances far beyond your control, why don't you invite me to do for you what you intend to teach the students that I will do for them? You are drained and frustrated, and you face an uncertain tomorrow. Let me nurture you now."

What could I say—"No, Lord, let's get practical here. Get my suitcases here by 8:00 A.M., that's really what I need"?

Wrong.

I yielded to the Lord's desire to love and nurture me. Feeling very alone while far from home, I accepted Jesus' invitation to come to him, and he embraced my entire situation. "Come to me, all you who are weary and burdened, and I will give you rest. Take my yoke upon you and learn from me . . . and you will find rest for your souls" (Matt. 11:28–29).

In those few hours Christ met me. My spirit was energized, my mind sharpened, and I felt physically refreshed. I got up and, with Bible and legal pad, shaped my opening day's material, both with new, fresh insights from the Lord's visit with me and from the memory of what I had already prepared. It was just short of astounding to me to see how the Spirit of Jesus empowered me to generate material for that opening class.

HARNESSING ENERGY

As I thought back on those first chaotic days in Ukraine shortly after my return to the States, I saw how God graciously, sovereignly, and wisely planned those few wearying and humiliating days in order to bring me, a very needy receiver of life, to Christ, who is Life. By his loving visitation, I was taken deeper and farther into the reality of his presence, and I became the recipient of his promised help. I experienced much more of the present Christ than I would have experienced without those pressing days. At Jesus' invitation I came to him on that cold Ukrainian night and took his yoke. He kept his word, and I found rest and renewal for my soul.

I spent a number of childhood years on my grandfather's farm in Bemis, Tennessee. I often saw him yoke together with a "single tree" a team of mules to plow the fields or pull a corn wagon. A yoke connects two animals in order to harness their energies for a working purpose. For training purposes a young, untrained mule is yoked to the older, stronger seasoned mule in order to break him in and harness his abilities. The younger may try to wander off, but the older pulls him along; the younger may lag behind or try to bolt ahead, but the older keeps him at a steady pace.

"Take my yoke," Jesus says,[1] which in effect means, "Connect with me for learning and training purposes. Imitate me in all that you do. I will be next to you, the wiser, stronger, seasoned one who will impart to you all that I am." The yoke metaphor makes Jesus' name "Immanuel" ("God with us") operative in our lives and ministries and makes his presence perceptible and profound in daily pastoral reality.

> *The yoke metaphor makes Jesus' name "Immanuel" ("God with us") operative in our lives and ministries and makes his presence perceptible and profound in daily pastoral reality.*

"Immanuel" moves us clearly into the yoked, supernatural presence of Jesus. While Jesus was renewing me in Ukraine—I was in a different time zone on the other side of the planet—he was also visiting Julie, my wife. Jesus was meeting her in deeply transforming ways through the teaching and prayer ministry of Dr. Victor Matthews. After one of the Wednesday evening sessions in our church, I got a call from Julie late in my Ukrainian night. She told how she was thrilled by God's visitation to her. I could tell in her voice that God had met her in new, refreshing ways.

For many reasons Julie has struggled with sensing God's love as a Father. Because of my own past struggles with this reality, I have not been the best one to lead her into the experience of God's life-changing love. As a graduate of Moody Bible Institute and a capable and informed Christian leader, Julie *knows* that God loves her, but how does that love move from her head to her heart?[2] Only about eighteen inches separate the head from heart, but it may as well be a million light years distance if a person does not *experience* the love of God. Julie was calling to tell me of God's love embarking on that miraculous eighteen-inch journey. "We cannot be loved without being changed. When people experience love, . . . they begin to grow lovely."[3] Here's how Julie journaled her experience with God that night:

> *I realized that I had believed powerful errors about myself. I thought my self-worth was dependent upon what I had, how I looked, and how I measured up compared to others. I believed God's message to me was: "You don't measure up, so shape up or else." But I realized tonight that God's truth was: "I want you, Julie, so come. Open your heart to me and receive my love." When Victor prayed these truths into me, God's love overpowered me and began a deep healing in my life.*

After the phone call, as I lay in bed in Ukraine, I marveled at *the presence*, the Immanuel nature of our Christ! God with me, God with Julie, God with each of his own. Fully, compassionately, and lovingly present.

This promised presence of Christ—this being yoked with him— is the vital dynamic of authentic pastoral work. The Timeless One is connected to the specific minutes and locations of our lives, our relationships, and our ministries.

THE VERY PRESENCE OF GOD

Jesus' presence with us is so much more than just the theology of omnipresence. The yoke speaks of the promised, imparted, perceptible presence of Jesus to and in his own. We are called into a salvation that includes visitations of God. The promises that God makes to his own children speak of a protecting, providing, and confidence-inspiring presence. When God declares, "Never will I leave you; never will I forsake you" (Heb. 13:5), surely he is doing more than just affirming his omnipresence.

In the manifest presence of God, he makes himself known in specific, sometimes surprising ways. "The Presence and the manifestation of the Presence are not the same. There can be one without the other. God is here when we are wholly unaware of it. He is *manifest* only when and as we are aware of His Presence. On our part there must be surrender to the Spirit of God, for His work it is to show us the Father and the Son."[4] I am coming to understand that the gifts of the Spirit are strategies that make manifest the very presence of God. Why should it surprise us that a supernatural God would use *supernatural gifts* to make himself known?

To reduce the promises of Jesus' "manifest presence" to meaning only his omnipresence, is to gut any meaning from the yoke metaphor. Omnipresence, on the one hand, means that Jesus as God is just as much "present" to the sincere Hindu priest, Buddhist monk, New Age guru, Muslim Shiite, Ukrainian atheist, rock, pear, and lizard as he is to his own "brothers and sisters" or with his "undershepherds." Taking the yoke, on the other hand, is more than affirming this doctrine of omnipresence. It is an intentional surrender to him who is ready *to impart his life and skills* to us, to make himself known in the particulars of our lives and ministries. We become eager apprentices of his character (who he is) and his ministry (the way he works). We begin to learn the way he "pulls the load" that we define as pastoral ministry in this world.

"Learn *from* me" cannot be reduced to "Learn *about* me." I can learn *about* carpentry from a book, but I can *become* a carpenter when I am guided by a skilled carpenter who says, as my stepfather, Neal, said when I was a teen, "Watch me, John. Do it like this." I am learning *of* Christ as I am learning *from* him.

I am not, by the way, a skilled carpenter, but one summer while on a missions trip to Trinidad with about sixteen adults from our church, I was assigned to build a new pantry in the camp kitchen. A good friend who is a professional builder was on the missions team. He supplied me with tools, walked me through the basics, and guided my work. I was in training.

"John, watch me."

Because I accepted my friend's "yoke" and learned of him as well as from him, I did something good—I built a decent pantry with sturdy shelves. I was very pleased, as were the camp personnel and my friend who trained and guided me. It was a job, thankfully, well done.

"Well done." Aren't those the words we long to hear Jesus say to us as we enter into glory? "Well done, good and faithful servant." When we take Jesus' yoke and learn from him, we begin to live and minister the way he did. Pastoral "well done" work is not grounded in cleverness, talent, experience, or doctrinal precision, though all these things have a place in our lives and ministry. "Well done" ministry is grounded in an intimate relationship with Jesus Christ and a courageous submission to live and minister the way he did. With intimacy and submission on our part, the Spirit empowers us to shepherd like the Chief Shepherd did (and does). Anything less will not be "well done," but half-baked.

Pastoring in the new millennium is going to require sharp-eyed apprentices who will watch Jesus work and do what he did. How can we keep a sharp eye on Jesus? By saturating our hearts and minds with the Gospels. We read, study, meditate, and dream the vision of ministry incarnate in Jesus Christ. We watch him deal with friends, enemies, the rich, poor, educated, and common.

> *"Well done" ministry is grounded in an intimate relationship with Jesus Christ and a courageous submission to live and minister the way he did.*

We listen to what he valued and what he detested. All the while, we accept God's purpose for us that we are to live as Jesus did. "I tell you the truth, anyone who has faith in me will do what I have been doing.

He will do even greater things than these, because I am going to the Father" (John 14:12).

Tired and frustrated from not catching any fish in the night, Peter and the other disciples were preparing to stretch out their nets for drying and repairing. Jesus walked up, surveyed the situation, and urged them to move out into deeper waters and cast their nets for a haul of fish. Peter initially protested but finally gave in, perhaps to teach Jesus a lesson—that Peter knew more about fishing than Jesus did. To everyone's surprise, including Peter's, the nets filled with fish.

Peter had one of his many "existential encounters" with Christ after that great catch of fish. Jesus is brilliant. He not only knows about fishing for men; he knows about fishing for fish too. So Peter learned the lesson: When Jesus is with us and tells us to do something, it is— to our happy but not necessarily easy surprise—a good thing to do what he says.

RISKING THE RIDE

One Sunday morning I had, as I normally do, a message prepared for a series I was preaching. As we worshiped, I kept thinking back on an experience of taking my family to a huge field to watch several hot-air balloons stretched out on the grass being prepared for inflation. It was a fascinating sight as the heaters with powerful fans filled the bright-colored canopies with air. They billowed up and rose several stories high. Passengers filled the gondolas, and away the balloons soared into the sky. These images filled my mind. Why?

I sensed that the Lord wanted me to go out into some deep water and do the unexpected thing. Mumbling like Peter, I said, "But Lord, I've toiled for days with this message." Did Jesus really want me to cast it aside? I wrestled with the reality of his real "yoked" presence and decided to do the risky thing.

In the space of a few minutes, I created a new message using the analogy of the beautiful hot-air balloon as a picture of our lives, of our church. I stepped up, told the church that I was going to do something different from what was on their bulletin outline, and did it.

People and churches, like hot-air balloons, have all the rigging (ministry structures), have the bright colors (visual appeal), have crew and passengers (leaders and followers), have huge fields for take off and landing (church-growth specified parking lots), and have all the mechanisms for operation (right doctrines and strategies). We have everything except fire. What we lack, I said, is the courage to fire up that little unit that heats up the ordinary and the obvious (air) and makes the whole thing function as a gorgeous, floating work of art. For our lives and churches, the heating unit is the Spirit of God— the fire. I called the church to an authentic relationship with the Spirit so that we may go wherever he (the wind also) may take us. However it turns out and wherever we go, it will be risky yet quite a ride!

To this day I will occasionally have someone in the church remind me of that sermon and the day I risked giving it. God used it to touch listeners' lives in a meaningful way. Can pastoral ministry have that kind of immediacy and creativity to it? Certainly, but not all the time. Yet at times the Chief Shepherd reserves the right to say to us, "I am stepping in to do my unexpected thing today. Are you ready?"

A generation of pastors is emerging whose flaming desire is to be yoked with Christ and to do what he did. If he grounded his identity in Scripture, these pastors will too. If he ministered in the supernatural power of the Holy Spirit, then these pastors will too by means of all the gifts of the Spirit given to the church. If he demonstrated deep-felt compassion that prompted merciful and caring conversations and actions (as well as good "sermons"), so will these pastors. If he practiced the spiritual disciplines as means of identity formation and ministry empowerment, so will these pastors in the new millennium find themselves getting alone with God in solitude and silence, passionately loving God and receiving ministry from him just as Jesus did. If Jesus engaged in spiritual warfare in his salvation-bringing work, so will empowered pastors of the twenty-first century put on the full armor of God and stand against the Enemy who prowls about deceiving and destroying people. As Martin Luther put it,

> Did we in our own strength confide,
>   our striving would be losing,
> Were not the right man on our side,
>   the man of God's own choosing.
> Dost ask who that may be?
>   Christ Jesus, it is he;
> Lord Sabbaoth, his name,
>   from age to age the same,
> and he must win the battle.

> We all, no matter our theology of gifts, long for more of the Giver than his gifts, for more of his presence than his power, for more of his Shepherd's heart beating in and through ours.

Jesus is not only *on* our side so that we can face the battle of ministry knowing his support and affirmation. Jesus, the Great and Chief Shepherd, is *by* our side so that we can draw upon his skill and wisdom. Even more compelling is the truth that Christ is *in* us empowering us to live as he did.

I have discovered the reality of Jesus' promised presence giving meaning to the particulars of my life and ministry. While significant dimensions of spiritual empowerment are enjoyed or forfeited based on one's "view of the gifts," I believe we all, no matter our theology of gifts, long for more of the Giver than his gifts, for more of his presence than his power, for more of his Shepherd's heart beating in and through ours.

Experiencing Christ is the primary and compelling mission of this book for pastors. In presenting my journey into new dimensions of empowerment, I am longing for pastors to reclaim their "first love," the Lord Jesus Christ. The risen Christ, whom we adore in worship and serve in pastoral work, promises to impart to each pastor those essential qualities of the Shepherd ascribed to David in Psalm 78:72: "David shepherded them with integrity of heart; with skillful hands he led them." This vision of shepherding calls us to a life and ministry of compassion.

JESUS AND COMPASSION

The Heart of the Pastoral Vision

My wife, Julie, while on a weekend retreat with the women of our church, was invited by the retreat speaker to minister pastorally to the women. Women, most of whom Julie has known for years, were prayed over and encouraged. During this time of ministry to others, God was visiting my wife in new and renewing ways. Julie was becoming less self-conscious of her incessant feelings of inferiority and inadequacy. God's great love had wrapped Julie in a blanket of security and value. Now, God's love *for others* was being "poured out into [Julie's] heart by the Holy Spirit" (see Romans 5:5). Julie was actually experiencing to a degree some of the wonder described by C. S. Lewis in *That Hideous Strength* that we spoke of in chapter 4. She was seeing herself through God's eyes and grasping her new identity as an empowered daughter of God.

Julie now entered into joyful service, loving women as a Spirit-anointed shepherd. Julie was discovering her own God-given identity and the selected flock for whom she was to care.

A gifted young wife and mother, whom we'll call Angela, was worshiping the Lord in a riveting interpretive dance, and Julie felt deep, gripping pangs of compassion for her. Delicate and graceful, fluid and beautiful, Angela had a personal history scarred with memories of horrible abuse, but Jesus had been meeting her and setting her free, "turning her mourning into dancing."

People respond to experiences of God-given compassion, such as my wife was undergoing, in different ways. Julie was actually doubled over with pangs of godly compassion. Julie would never conclude that her compassionate reactions toward Angela are the standard for all to experience. How individuals process deep feelings of compassion vary, and there is no formula for "doing compassion right."

I remember an evening in 1972 when I was working the night shift as a hospital orderly while a student at Dallas Seminary. I was so taken by the medical profession that I was thinking of transferring to medical school to become a medical missionary. I had read the story of Paul Carlson, a captive missionary doctor in the Congo, who was gunned down on November 24, 1964, while trying to scale a wall during a rescue operation. I wanted to take his place in the world and advance the cause of Christ. Should I stay in seminary or go to medical school?

This particular evening an attractive young woman came into the emergency room nicely dressed but violently beat up. Her lips were split and bloody, an eye was swelling shut, her forehead had abrasions, and the front of her blouse was ripped. She was in pain. I sat by her while the nurse went to get the night-duty emergency room doctor.

The patient and I were left in the emergency room alone. I asked her what happened. She told me that she and her husband were at a bar for the evening where he got drunk and became violently angry with her in the parking lot. He hit her in the face and threw her to the pavement, then got in the car and drove away, leaving her on the pavement. Some bypassers found her and brought her to the emergency room.

As she spoke, the patient began to cry. When I asked if her injuries were causing her pain, she said, "No, it's not my cuts. I am afraid, but I am not afraid of what he did to me." She sobbed deeply and blurted out, "I am so afraid of what he is doing to my children right now." My heart went out to her. In the face of her own physical agony, her greatest pain was fear—fear for her children being battered by a drunk, angry man.

The doctor swept into the room and took over. He cleaned her injuries, stitched her cut lips, and asked a lot of questions about *her body*. Then the doctor left—swift, efficient, done. Bewildered by the two levels of pain in her life—physical and relational—I felt something deep within me forming a question, "But who will doctor *her soul?*" Right then, feeling great compassion for the woman's plight welling up within me, I decided to stay in seminary and learn the ancient biblical art known as "the cure of the soul."[1] I'm glad I made that choice, but over the years I have discovered that most of what I learned in seminary had little to do with preparing me to deal with a battered woman fearing for the well-being of her children. Very little direction was offered for empowerment to address that kind of situation. As Howard Hendricks often told us as students, "You'll be four years in seminary, and it'll take you eight years to get over it."[2]

A HEART FOR PEOPLE

Deep-felt compassion is one of the primary and controlling emotions of pastoral ministry. Jesus felt it and, as Chief Shepherd, modeled it for all who would pastor. This emotion is visceral and compels action. It is the human expression of *the heart of God* for people.

Jesus gazed across the Galilean hillsides and saw multitudes of people seeking to draw near to him and his disciples. Matthew writes that as Jesus' eyes scanned the crowds, he "had *compassion* on them, because they were harassed and helpless, like *sheep without a shepherd* " (Matt. 9:36, italics mine). Matthew records the connection between Jesus' deep-felt pangs of compassion and his declaration for the need of pastoral leadership.

> *Deep-felt compassion is one of the primary and controlling emotions of pastoral ministry. Jesus felt it and, as Chief Shepherd, modeled it for all who would pastor.*

The term for compassion in Matthew 9:36 makes an interesting study. A form of the Greek verb *splanchnizomai*, it is based on a noun meaning "inward parts," "entrails," or our colloquial word "guts."[3] It sometimes refers to the kidneys and liver and other vital organs taken out of some Old Testament sacrificial animals and eaten by priests and others. The word evolved as a verb meaning "to feel deep passion for." These deep feelings were thought to be localized in the lower inner organs. Strong emotions such as courage, compassion, righteous anger, and mercy originated in the inward parts. The opposite idea, "cowardice," was communicated by adding the letter "a" to the beginning of the word (the alpha primitive) to create the term "without inward parts," or more bluntly "no guts."

Jesus used the term *splanchnizomai* for deep-felt compassion in three of his well-known parables. Those three stories are: (1) The debtor and the king (Matt. 18), in which compassion provokes forgiveness of a huge debt, teaching us that compassion has priority over and is the source of forgiveness. (2) The good Samaritan (Luke 10), a parable in which Jesus, with incredible courage, addresses his Jewish audience's deep racial prejudice as he ascribes compassion to the "good Samaritan" in contrast to the Jewish priest and Levite, thereby making a deeply despised Samaritan the hero of the story. (3) The prodigal son (Luke 15), a story in which compassion compels the returning prodigal's father to act in unexpected loving ways toward his "found" son.

Jesus liked to use this "gut-level" word, *splanchnizomai*. Moreover, Jesus lived out this word as Chief Shepherd in his ministry to the diseased, demonized, and marginalized. Consider the encounter with the leper.

One day as Jesus and his followers were going from village to village, a leper bolted out of the shadows, raced to Jesus, and fell at his feet crying out, "Sir, if you are willing, you can make me clean!" Put this scene on "pause" for a moment. We know that the Mosaic code forbade what this leper was doing. He was commanded to wear unkempt hair and scream "Unclean!" whenever around healthy people. In other words, he was to send out both visual and verbal signals so that healthy people would stay away.

Healthy persons would never touch a leper for fear of contracting the disease or becoming ceremonially unclean themselves. Strong biblical commands and stringent community mores kept lepers quarantined. Jewish tradition even commanded that lepers could not be upwind from well people. The thinking behind this rule was that the wind would blow across the leper and downwind onto the healthy, and they would be contaminated.

Imagine the shock, then, to the followers of Jesus to have this maniac leper leap into their circle and fall at Jesus' feet. Mosaic law and Jewish teaching were being blatantly defied. What would the rabbi do?

Jesus did not scream, "What in the world are you doing? Get out of here! You are violating the law and risking my friends' lives. You know the rules and you broke them. We never heard you cry, 'Unclean!' I'm going to summon the religious police and have you arrested." No, Jesus did none of that.

I think Jesus truly admired the do-or-die risk this leper took to get to him. Jesus looked into that desperate man's eyes and saw the searing pain of alienation.

Lepers were alienated from family and friends, cut off from community. Lepers were alienated from their own bodies. Their disease-mutilated and smelly flesh became hostile to everything human beings hold dear. Most tragically, lepers were alienated from God. Prevailing opinion in Jesus' day was that leprosy was a curse from God. We cannot fathom the sense of isolation lepers experienced. They were literally alone in the universe, abandoned in every significant relationship.

What would the rabbi do? Jesus read the consuming aloneness in this leper's face, the alienation that permeated his soul. Jesus felt compassion[4] for the leper. Moved deeply by this man's horrible plight, Jesus himself did the unthinkable: he touched the leper. Jesus violated the Mosaic law too! Why? To demonstrate that mercy triumphs over justice. Compassion supersedes command when human life is in jeopardy. He touched the leper with hands of compassion. Imagine—this was the first human touch this leper had felt in years! Not only did Jesus touch; he also spoke. "I am willing. Be cleansed!" Mark records that immediately the leper was healed.

With deep-felt emotion, a daring touch, and the authoritative word, Jesus supernaturally reunited this man to God, to his family and friends, and to his now cleansed body. Sin (symbolized by leprosy) divides, alienates. Salvation integrates, unites. Jesus is God's anointed agent of salvation.

MAY I HAVE THIS DANCE?

Our worship team was asked to do a concert at one of the inner-city ministries for the homeless and socially marginalized in Grand Rapids. Julie and I went along to help serve meals. After everyone had eaten and during the time of celebrative singing, I noticed an elderly woman, looking like a classic bag lady, wanting to dance. She was unkempt to say the least—disheveled hair, missing teeth, weathered skin, and as I soon found out, she smelled horrible.

Welling up within me was a compulsion to ask her for the next dance. Would this be proper? I asked one of the directors of the place if she thought it would be okay if I asked "the bag lady" to dance. "She'd love it," I was told. During the pause between songs, I went over to her, introduced myself, and asked her to dance. The next song was a slower tempo, so I put my arm around her and she put hers on my shoulder.

As we started to dance, she smiled sweetly at me (missing teeth and all), and then in my arms, she drifted away, seemingly lost in some long-forgotten memories. I wondered, *Is this what Jesus would do for this lady?* Yes, it seemed so right to bring a moment of joy and affirmation, of acceptance and delight to this woman, to create just one more memory for her that told her she was a woman of beauty and worth.

On the following Sunday, one of our worship band members came to me. "John, you know what made that evening for me in the inner city?"

"What?" I asked.

"When you, my pastor, asked that dirty, old lady for a dance. Your willingness to show that kind of love made me realize how good our God is. John, you made that evening wonderful for her. Thanks for the courage and love it took to do that."

Think of the good Samaritan. Why would Jesus create in his story a despised Samaritan as the hero who "felt compassion" on the near dead victim on the Jericho road (Luke 10)? Because Jesus himself deeply loved those most despised and most desperate in the world and, amazingly, as a Jew, Jesus was willing to be identified with the "good" Samaritan.

Think of the Samaritan woman at the well. She learned personally in a one-on-one conversation with Jesus that he was her long-awaited Messiah, and he invited her into the circle of true worshipers of the Father. Her being a *woman* did not stop Jesus from treating her with deep respect by conversing with her publicly. (Public discourse with women was forbidden by Jewish law as being sexually inappropriate.) Her being a *Samaritan* woman did not stop Jesus from treating her with affirming dignity even though she was culturally a "half-breed," contaminated by Assyrian blood. Her being a theological heretic did not stop Jesus from engaging her in a serious and meaningful dialogue on theological issues. (Samaritans only considered their sectarian version of the Pentateuch as binding Scripture, and they erected a temple to rival the temple in Jerusalem.) Her being immoral and living in immorality did not stop Jesus from addressing her as a human being with as much opportunity to become a worshiper of God as any other person. Every conceivable barrier that stops most believers today, even many pastors, from conversing with others about the Christian hope is blown away by Christ as he meets people with compassion. Sexual gender differences, racial differences, theological differences, and moral differences—none of these mattered most to Jesus. Why? Because the *person* mattered more.[5]

Like Jesus, we must not meet people with only doctrine in our head, ready to communicate and excommunicate, but with a God-given compassion that sees the potential for every human being to become a worshiper of the Father in spirit and truth. Most people are alert to manipulated religious conversations that go for the "gospel kill" but show little care for them as persons.

Lee Strobel is a pastor who models being moved with compassion. In his book *What Jesus Would Say*, Lee imagines Jesus speaking to Madonna, the popular singer who is known for her blatant immoral and antireligious behavior. Whereas many pastors use Madonna as a sermonic whipping post to rail against the downward spiral of pop culture, Strobel seriously tries to imagine what Jesus' approach to and dialogue with Madonna would be. With the "woman at the well" (John 4) in the background of his thinking, Strobel imagines Jesus speaking to Madonna. As Strobel documents, Madonna is driven by her need for personal affirmation and worth, worth she draws from her fans. Jesus would say to her:

> I understand what happens when I'm missing from the core of a person's life. I understand how you feel compelled to search elsewhere for significance, affirmation, acceptance, self-worth, fulfillment, and love. That search has taken you to some dangerous and destructive places—and you still haven't found what you're looking for. You see, the frustration you feel is because the only thing that can satisfy the center of your soul is Me.[6]

The very people we are most tempted to criticize and condemn, Jesus is ready to show compassion and treat with great conversational respect.

Compassion "makes the unbounded mercy of God visible. . . . [It] expresses the attitude of complete willingness to use all means, time, strength, and life, for saving at the crucial moment."[7] When Julie ached with a deep-felt mercy and love for Angela, she was making visible what God the Father felt for Angela. Julie felt the pastoral drive to enter into Angela's life with a message of blessing, a touch of grace, an embrace of love, affirming Angela as a person and celebrating her giftedness.

Commenting on Jesus' compassion for people who were like sheep without a shepherd, Davies and Allison say, "Undoubtedly in this, as in so much else, Jesus is implicitly being presented as a model for Christian behavior."[8] If Christian behavior includes gut-level feelings of mercy, making God's heart visible, then surely pastors who are having Christ formed in them must model a radical compassion.

> *If Christian behavior includes gut-level feelings of mercy, making God's heart visible, then surely pastors who are having Christ formed in them must model a radical compassion.*

MORE THAN PREACHING

Where will pastors get this kind of compassion? One thing is for sure: we cannot manufacture it or conjure it up at will. We might try to pretend it, but pretense will not sustain us over the pastoral long haul. This deep and genuine pastoral response must come from one source: the Chief Shepherd, Jesus Christ. Helmut Kosser, commenting on the apostle Paul's use of the term *splanchnizomai*, states, "This kind of love and affection which grip and profoundly move the whole man are possible only in Christ."[9] Such profound compassion grasps the reality of people's "harassed and helpless" condition (Matt. 9:36), responds inwardly and powerfully, and takes compassionate action to make a change for the better. Compassion is the heart (or "inward parts") of pastoring.

By contrast, I was trained to consider *the sermon*—an act of communication—as the heart of the pastoral ministry. Everything was to revolve around the priority of message preparation and delivery. The idea inherent in this pastoral vision is that people need information, truth, "doctrine in the frontal lobe," meaty, expository messages.

As I mentioned earlier, I am a pastor and I have the spiritual gift of teaching. Appropriately, according to my spiritual gifts, I serve as the teaching pastor in our church. I was trained in what I think is the best seminary for learning the art of expository preaching, so I am not belittling message preparation or delivery. I do it every week of the year except for about four to six Sundays, and I preach three times on Sunday morning. I highly enjoy this significant aspect of the pastoral task, but it is not the heart of pastoring.

I like to think of the people coming into the services carrying not only a Bible, but also a map of their souls. Preaching helps people not only to "know the Bible," but to acquaint them with the revelatory landscape of their inner lives. People need training in reading the maps of their spiritual journey and guidance for those rendezvous points where they may meet God. Most people (and maybe many pastors) are unaware of the uncharted terrain of the soul and are unskilled in grasping the geography of the inner life. Preaching opens people's eyes to the vast horizons of the kingdom of God *within* them as well as pointing people toward the work that God is doing around them.

Pastoring, by contrast, is moving out from behind the pulpit and into the lives of harassed and helpless people, bringing God to them in the ordinary time and space particulars of their lives. Pastoring, as earlier defined, is bringing God to people. The pastor, having described the map of the soul in preaching, now serves as an "up close and personal" spiritual guide into that vast inner terrain.

It is here that most Bible expositors make ineffective pastors. Disciples, men and women who are being transformed to live like Jesus, cannot be mass produced. "Nondiscipleship is the elephant in the church."[10] It takes time and patient compassion to bring God to people in the particulars of their lives so that Christ is formed in them. Of course, pastors cannot do this task alone, nor should they. Yet it is pastors who are called to the task of making it possible for the people in their charge to experience God. Pastors help people *experience* Immanuel.

Is that not what the Chief Shepherd did? Jesus is the incarnate Word, or as a child says, "God with skin on." As undershepherds, pastors also bring God to people, not just in preached word (communication), but also in deeply felt, Spirit-imparted love that acts on their behalf (compassion).

The people in Jesus' day had "good Bible teaching." Scripture was valued, studied, and taught in the synagogue. The people also had plenty of religious leaders and political rulers—Pharisees, Sadducees, the Herods, Roman centurions, Pilate. Jesus saw what the people had, and he also saw what they did not have—pastors. In the absence of shepherds, the people, like shepherdless sheep, wandered harassed and helpless. Feeling compassion for people saved Jesus from the devastating turmoil that many pastors easily fall into: anger, resignation, boredom, condescension, and burnout.

I have heard too many angry men and women passing themselves off as pastors. Anger, one of the seven deadly sins, creates enemies and then tries to destroy them, but "the Lord's servant must not quarrel; instead, he must be kind to everyone, able to teach, not resentful" (2 Tim. 2:24). Resentful anger emerges and builds in those pastors who realize over time that what they accepted as a mighty calling has turned out to be, at times, a dull, irritating job, a job that is often thankless and underpaid. "If there is anything that makes ministry look grim and dull, it is this dark, insidious anger in the servants of Christ."[11]

Pastors also readily discover that preaching exquisite biblical sermons and being the public relations "nice guy" isn't creating stalwart saints or empowered laity. Dashed expectations provoke anger that is often held inside until it blows out sideways in addictions or affairs. More often the anger is taken out on the spouse, children, and dog. Anger leads pastors to resign, either literally or emotionally.

Some pastors outright quit, forsaking their calling; others quit, too, but stay in the pastorate, faking their calling. Far from the hearts of pastors like these is any semblance of compassion.

Other diseased attitudes set in that contaminate pastoral relationships. Boredom and condescension, according to Eugene Peterson, are the twin results of pastors who cease seeing ordinary and sometimes irritable people as major characters in God's story of salvation.[12] People can become tediously boring to the Hebrew and Greek trained, exegetically minded, expository message bearing, culturally relevant communicator of biblical truth. It is easy for such an enlight-ened, sermon-charged person to be (im)patiently condescending to those scruffy ones who desperately need the Word exegeted for them.

Peterson points out, on the other hand, that even the most difficult and stubborn people are not to be resisted by pastors. Empowered by the compassion of Christ, a pastor is on the prowl to discover how each individual in his or her charge is part of and actually perpetuates God's fasci-nating story of exhilarating grace. Every detail of their lives can be a clue left by the unseen and passionate Lover of their souls. Pastors are detectives searching for the fingerprints of God on peoples' lives.

> *Pastors are detec-tives searching for the fingerprints of God on peoples' lives.*

FILLING THE GAPING HOLE

In my ministry the time came when my patchwork quilt of pastoral vision shredded. I came to dread, even detest, Sundays. The moments I hated most were those after the singing and just before the message when I had to reach down and turn on the FM sending unit of my lapel microphone. I had become a cold, professionally prepared ser-mon machine. People continued to affirm my "good Bible teaching," and thankfully God did bless his faithfully declared Word. But I had become at heart just a communication device with as little feeling as my microphone's sending unit. I had become just another piece of the *technology* of communication, and I deeply resented it.

What changed me? Or, more accurately, *who* changed me? Jesus did. How? By conveying his gut-level compassion for me. When I asked God to tell me the purpose of the "Grand Canyon" in my soul left by my father's absence and God responded, "That gaping hole is there so I, your heavenly Father, can fill it," I melted into a vast sor-row mingled with an even more vast wonder. I was feeling, literally in my inward parts, the great compassion and wisdom of God in writing even the wretched and wrecked particulars of my life into his grand, sweeping story of redemption. Jesus met me in those moments, telling me that he was not ashamed to call me his brother. Jesus and I had and could enjoy together the same Father. I was almost delirious in the thrill of it all.

God's gut-level love restored to me an intense passion for him, a new love for people, and an absolute overhaul of what it meant for me to be a pastor. In Christ, not only am *I* deeply loved, but I receive the love of the Chief Shepherd *for his sheep.* Jesus literally shepherded me, a harassed and helpless man, modeling for me in my own life experience what pastoring is really all about.

During the days of these profound personal changes, I moved into the exegetical certainty that all the gifts of the Spirit given to the church (Rom. 12; 1 Cor. 12–14; Eph. 4; 1 Peter 4) are still being given and are operable today. I entered into the experience of those gifts personally, either using some of them myself or receiving the benefits of them as they were lovingly directed to me through others.

Eugene Peterson's forged metal of the pastoral vision as presented in *Five Smooth Stones* erupted into living expression, and I entered, perhaps for the first time, genuine pastoral ministry. Oh, I still preach. I still turn on the lapel microphone, but I do so filled with the experiential reality of God's love, not just an exegetical message of God's truth. People respond not only with affirming words about the teaching ministry, but by reporting that they are being pastored as well. I am not only bringing them truth from God; I am guiding them to an encounter with God. Am I saying that preaching itself cannot bring God to people? No, I am not trying to build a great wall between preaching and pastoring, but I am saying that pastoring includes more than preaching.

Pastoral ministry is fueled by God's gut-level, experiential love. Eugene Peterson notes, "All truth must be experienced personally before it is complete, before it is authentic."[13] When Peter, Jesus' friend and disciple, having shamefully denied Jesus three times, tried to bail out of Christ's calling on his life, what did Jesus ask three times over their seaside breakfast together? He asked, "Peter, do you love me?" (see John 21:15–19).

When Jesus called those disillusioned disciples to come and eat with him, he was saying to them that he still deeply respected them, that he still welcomed them as equals, and that he still wanted to honor them.[14] Jesus' invitation to Peter was: "Peter, I know all about your denials. I know you better than you know yourself. Come, my friend, eat with me. We're partners. Let's shepherd together. Peter, do you love me?"

Peter replied, "Lord, you know everything. You know I love you."

Jesus, in wonder of all wonders, said, "Peter, feed my sheep."

"Do you love me?" asks Jesus. Every pastor must answer that question with integrity. Compassion, Christ's activated love, received and given away to harassed and helpless people, is the heart of empowered pastoral ministry. Anything less, good as it may be, cannot be called pastoring.

A few years ago some church staff members and I attended a Pastoral Counseling Ministry seminar at Wheaton College led by Leanne Payne and her staff. A prolific writer and engaging speaker, Leanne Payne leads a ministry that addresses the horrific struggles of those in bondage to sexually addictive lifestyles. Some of our church staff had read Leanne's books and had heard about her ministry. We decided to go and see for ourselves what she and her ministry were like.

> *Compassion, Christ's activated love, received and given away to harassed and helpless people, is the heart of empowered pastoral ministry.*

During one of the evening sessions, after a stimulating lecture, Leanne called, without any hype whatsoever, for the Spirit to come and apply Jesus' redeeming work to specific sins and bondages in people's lives. She simply prayed, "Holy Spirit, come." The Spirit came in great liberating power, and I was in awe of God's working. As I observed this ministry, I became restless, wanting so strongly to be able to minister to those who needed prayer and encouragement. But I was just an attendee, not a team member, and only authorized team members were to serve those in need.

At one point, however, I noticed a young man who, while we were singing, held his arms out and up toward God, crying as he sang his love to God. He did this for a long time. Soon his arms began to sag, and he struggled to keep them raised. My heart went out to this young man, this stranger who appeared to be receiving God's love and returning it in tender and tearful praise. I felt compassion for him, a strong inner emotion to help, so I moved next to him and helped him keep his arms raised to the Lord.

When the song ended, he turned and fell in my arms and sobbed into my shoulder and neck. I just held him in my embrace as he cried and cried. After about five minutes, he pulled back and turned to worship as the singing continued. After the ministry time and as we were leaving, this young man moved next to me and said, "As I was in your arms, I felt the love of God *as my Father* for the first time in my life. I felt your masculine cheek against mine, and in that touch, I received affirmation from God about his acceptance of me as a man. Thank you."

Can you believe it? I, with no father model, wounded by a Grand Canyon–sized father abandonment, was so filled with father love by the Holy Spirit that it spilled over into this young man. I truly pastored. I brought God the Father to that abandoned soul. I have just one word for it: *miracle.*

God is helping me clarify my purpose in life: to help people *experience* God as Father. I told the young man that his kind words affirmed why I exist. We rejoiced together. Compassion and pastoral ministry are inseparable.

How do pastors receive Christ's shepherd's heart? How can they, out of their bonding to Christ, experience and express pastoral compassion? Only through the practice of the spiritual disciplines—the topic of the next chapter.

JESUS AND THE SPIRITUAL DISCIPLINES

THE PRIORITY OF PASTORAL MINISTRY

OUR assignment for the weekend was to experience a silent retreat. That may sound quite tame, but we were a group of very talkative doctor of ministry students—pastors and Christian leaders from various denominations—in Fuller Theological Seminary's "Christian Spirituality" track. Silence, indeed, would be a hard discipline for some of us. And since confession is good for the soul, I might as well admit it here for all to read—a few of us cheated. Being experienced and professional talkers, we just couldn't take it anymore. One night in a hide-away stair landing, we broke the silence. Big time. Now that I've confessed, I feel so much better.

Anyway, we were learning about the disciplines of the spiritual life, and now, on this weekend retreat, teachings about solitude, silence, and meditation were to become real in our experience. Our spiritual guide for the weekend was a Claretian nun who loved Jesus Christ deeply and who guided us skillfully through, what turned out to be for me, a profound weekend.

At one point in the retreat, I went into the chapel of the Claretian retreat center to practice the discipline of Christian meditation. We were learning that a creative exercise in meditation is imagining and recording a dialogue with another person or even a thing. I sat in the chapel alone and silent. Suspended above the altar was a golden, beautifully detailed crucifix. It was not only a stunning work of art, but it became for me a focus of life-changing dialogue. I imagined and recorded a personal dialogue between the crucified Savior and me.

At first I felt sort of funny—kind of weird, actually. What's a good Protestant pastor doing meditating before a crucifix? The Holy Spirit, I truly believe, drew me beyond my sensitivities, and I began to imagine a conversation with Jesus while he hung on the cross for me. Mysteriously the Spirit of God entered into the dialogue at some point, and I was no longer imagining a conversation. A real conversation took place. In the discipline of meditation, the living Christ met me in a Catholic chapel before a golden crucifix. As the conversation unfolded, I was moved deeply.

The conversation was profound. I kept it to myself for the longest time, only mentioning *that* I had had a conversation with Christ, not *what* the conversation included. The Desert Fathers urged disciples not to speak of their encounters with God. Speech, like an open door on a stove, would let the fire out.

Later, as I was training others in our church in the spiritual disciplines, I sensed a freedom from God to relate the conversation to others. What follows is my journal entry of that provocative encounter with the crucified Christ.

AT THE CROSS
A Meditative Dialogue

John: Lord, I come to sit before you as you hang in agony upon the cross. I cannot tell the anguish, but I know you were there for me.

Jesus: This is why I came. See me here and know.

John: You did so many wonderful things, Lord. You spoke so much about the Father and the kingdom. You did so much for the poor, the diseased, the outcasts, the ones held captive by the Enemy of our lives.

Jesus: Small talk—that's all that was. See me now and hear the voice of God telling the magnificent message, the greatest act and word—the cross!

John: Does it hurt, Lord? I see the nails in your wrists and feet. Suspended on iron driven through flesh, the weight of your body pulls you down toward the earth.

Jesus: Don't dwell on the physical pain. See, there are two beside me who writhe in torturous pain as I do. In the physical pain I am not alone. Remember this.

John: There is a pain, then, of another kind, isn't there, Lord?

Jesus: Do you truly see it, John? Will you see it in me?

John: Oh, Lord, am I able? I fear that I am not or dare not be.

Jesus: Don't be afraid. This pain I bear is mine alone. The Sinless One now sin. The Living One ready to die. The Whole One broken. The Righteous One made repulsive to the Father. This is my pain—mine alone.

John: For me? Oh, Lord, for me?

Jesus: For you, John. Oh how I love you. So does my Father.

John: Lord, I see your hands. They did so much good. They built things; they pointed out things like flowers and birds; they blessed people—even little babies; they touched lepers and multiplied fish and bread; they stopped raging storms and invited sinners to eat with you. Now, Lord, they are torn and bloody, riveted into wood and soon to be still in death.

Jesus: My hands bless you, John, and some day will touch you. I will embrace you, my friend.

John: Your feet, Lord, angled on top of one another and nailed into the cross. Feet that have felt the fallen dust, the cool grass, the choppy waves, and the prostitute's tears and hair. Feet that stepped out of brilliant glory into sinful darkness and walked in my world. Feet that stumbled on the way to the cross. Beautiful feet that brought good news.

Jesus: Follow me.

John: Your body, exposed and abused, was prepared by the Father. In your body, O Christ, you did God's will until you could cry out, "It is finished!"

Jesus: It is. Yet I'm not finished with you, John.

John: I will stay a little longer, Lord. You have finished the work you came to do. Now I see you breathe your last breath, bow your head, and call out, "Father, into your hands I commit my spirit."

Jesus: Yes, my last movements as the Suffering Servant and Lamb of God.

John: You are still now. You appear, amid the awkward angles and blood, asleep. At rest. Still.

Jesus: Dead, John.

John: And can it be that you, my God, would die for me?

God: I did.

John: Thank you. I adore you, O crucified God! I bow down to you, slain Lamb of God. I take refuge in the cross of my Savior and my God!

A battered human body dangles on cross beams, still in death. Head bowed, eyes closed, still—very still. Heaven is so quiet. Angels gaze in wonder. Hell turns a curious and trembling eye toward Calvary. Friends weep and plunge into deepest despair. Enemies walk about congratulating themselves on a good day's work. Mary ponders the sword mark in her son's side and feels the gash in her own heart. Where is the Father? Has he forsaken his Son forever? Where is the Father whose Beloved hangs still, there on those bloody planks? See him there? Oh, do you see the Father there? He's the one on whose shoulder the head of Jesus rests in death. The Cross has become the Father's embrace! Hallelujah! Amen!

Some months later, after this retreat encounter with Christ, I was in conversation with a good friend, Kurt Dillinger. Kurt directs one of our nation's most innovative crisis pregnancy centers—the Pregnancy Resource Center of Grand Rapids. In the past Kurt and I have served together on our church's ministry team and have led adults on short-term mission trips to Trinidad and Tobago, West Indies. Kurt wanted to talk about an unusual struggle he was having.

Kurt had taken an adult team to Trinidad and, as part of the ministry, the team showed the *Jesus* film. Each time the film reached the crucifixion scene, Kurt would turn away from the screen. He could not bring himself to view the violence of Jesus' crucifixion. Kurt said that he finally forced himself to watch the crucifixion of Jesus as depicted in the film, but it still bothered him deeply. Thinking about physical violence or abuse of people caused great uneasiness in Kurt.

As we talked, Kurt's dilemma became apparent. The crucial event in our salvation from sin is Jesus' death on the cross. The apostle Paul boldly proclaimed Christ crucified as a core element in the powerful gospel message ("We preach Christ crucified," 1 Cor. 1:23). Kurt affirmed the necessity of the message of the cross—violent as a crucifixion is—but still found that he could not bring himself to even think about it.

I related to Kurt how Jesus met me in a time of meditation before the cross. I encouraged Kurt to go to a Catholic church that had a detailed crucifix and meditate on God's love as expressed in Jesus' death. Kurt found a church with a life-size crucifix, and he gazed upon it, meditating on Jesus' sacrificial love for him. God met Kurt in a powerful healing way.

Kurt told me later, "John, I knew that if I did not embrace the violence of the cross, then I would not be able to fully embrace God's love for me. When God broke through my extreme resistance to the violence of the cross, I experienced his love for me like I never have before."

Kurt's ministry at the Pregnancy Resource Center forces him daily to face the violence of abortion. "Somehow God's experience of violence in Christ at the cross has helped me and my staff as we daily engage with those who contemplate abortion and experience postabortion trauma. We constantly face the violence of abortion in our nation. The reality of the cross of Jesus is crucial for our effectiveness," Kurt said.

This conversation with Kurt cast me in the role of spiritual director, offering counsel that never would have been in my field of training had I not been trained myself. Pastoral ministry became an artful adventure as well as a theological profession. I don't expect to counsel everyone to meditate before a crucifix, but for Kurt it was very fitting. That spiritual exercise was meaningful *in the particulars* of his life and ministry.

Do we pastors even know about, much less enter into, the vast and varied relationships, practices, and experiences available to us and others to meet God? Spiritual disciplines are powerful resources that allow us to encounter God in powerful—and sometimes unusual—ways. I knew very little about the wide range of spiritual disciplines after my formal theological education. Now, like many Christians and Christian leaders, I'm playing catch-up. Like many, I came across the writings of Richard Foster.

> *Spiritual disciplines are powerful resources that allow us to encounter God in powerful — and sometimes unusual — ways.*

Little did I recognize that my first negative, even mildly hostile, reaction to reading Foster's *Celebration of Discipline* was more a commentary on the paltry state of my soul than on anything to do with his book. As I noted, nowhere in my entire theological education were the classical spiritual disciplines presented as serious practices for growth in grace. I had been told countless times to read my Bible and pray, and if I really wanted to be on the spiritual "A list," I should witness. That's it. Thus, reading Foster's call to practice many more disciplines sounded too much like work(s). Isn't growth in grace by faith and not "works"?

Now as I reread Foster or Dallas Willard's *The Spirit of the Disciplines*, I chuckle. I have a reaction similar to when I first read *Five Smooth Stones*. I say, "Where have I been all my life?" I had been so steeped in the Reformers' forensic paradigm of positional truth that any kind of effort exerted toward Christlikeness was considered antigrace and antifaith. Granted, my stagnant spiritual condition could very well have resulted from my own misunderstanding about my "position in Christ," yet I never was offered any spiritual direction beyond, "Read your Bible, pray every day, and witness."

When I first read about solitude and silence, submission and service, confession (do Protestants do confession?), meditation and journaling, celebration and fasting, I reacted negatively. I thought, *This sounds like "works salvation," which has an "earn your way to God" feel to it.*

Dallas Willard makes a provocative and wonderfully liberating observation when he declares that grace is opposed to earning, not effort. The spiritual disciplines take effort. "While none can merit salvation, all must act if it is to be theirs."[1] I had been *conditioned* to think effort meant earning. How wrong I was.

SPACE FOR GOD TO WORK

What is a spiritual discipline? It is simply a human activity that creates a space or setting for God to work. I do mean for *God to work* and work mightily. I now understand, for example, that solitude and silence are not activities that *earn* God's favor or blessing. They are simply practices I choose to do that position me *to receive* God's favor or blessing. Since this is true, I would be a fool to be negligent in practicing these two significant, time-honored behaviors.

I lived and pastored for years in both ignorance of and disobedience to most of the classical spiritual disciplines. After a while the flimsy cloth of my self-made pastoral vision began to shred, leaving me wondering why I seemed to have reached a barren and lifeless plateau in my growth in Christlikeness.

One startling reality about the spiritual disciplines is that Jesus Christ practiced them. The Chief Shepherd not only practiced them for himself; he practiced them as a pattern for us to follow. That is why I wrote above that I was *disobedient* with reference to the disciplines.

Dallas Willard did the church a remarkable service in calling us to seriously consider not only Jesus' teachings, but also *his very way of life.* Jesus' way of life models a consistent practice of the spiritual disciplines. Christlikeness without the practice of the disciplines is an absolute absurdity and impossibility.

Christlikeness—what an incredible concept! Think about it. The heavenly Father has purposed that his salvation shape us into the image of his Son (Rom. 8:29). "God's whole purpose, conceived in a past eternity, being worked for and in his people in history, to be completed in the glory to come, may be encapsulated in the single concept: *God intends to make us like Christ.*"[2]

Paul prayed and labored intently among Christians with the goal that Christ be formed in them (Gal. 4:19; Col. 1:28–29). But it is the apostle John who confronts believers with the divine moral imperative to live as Jesus lived: "Whoever claims to live in him must walk as Jesus did" (1 John 2:6).

If a person makes the claim that he or she lives in relationship to Jesus Christ—that is, that he or she is a Christ-follower, then that person is morally bound to "walk" as Jesus did. The term *walk* is common metaphor in the New Testament and means "to live a way of life."[3] Glenn Barker comments on 1 John 2:6, "The author is not claiming that the walk of Jesus can be perfectly imitated but that there is a divine imperative—which must be taken seriously for believers to live according to the way Jesus lived."[4]

As the searing truth of 1 John 2:6 sank into my soul, I was driven to the Gospels. This one verse alone compels every believer, and especially pastors, to ransack the Gospels, urgently asking, "How exactly did Jesus live?"

The purpose of the Gospels is to provide a twofold understanding of Jesus Christ. First, we discover what he taught. We hear him invite us into relationship with him and his Father and into the kingdom of God. We hear his descriptions of what his followers will be like. He was called "Rabbi," or Teacher. The Gospels record his messages, his parables, his public and private conversations, his debates with his opponents, and his farewell to his friends. He was both the embodiment and messenger of truth. John Ortberg writes that we must receive Jesus as Teacher as well as Savior.[5]

Second, we see how Jesus lived. We watch as he travels, touches, heals, sleeps, and eats. We do this so that not only can we say, "Jesus of Nazareth is the unique Son of God," but also so we can say, "Now I see how I am to live as a child of God within the kingdom of God." If we are true disciples (Dallas Willard suggests the term "apprentices") of Jesus Christ, when we are fully trained we will *be like our teacher* (Luke 6:40). Discipleship results not so much in Christian indoctrination ("getting the right answers"), as in Christlike transformation ("living the right life").[6]

The Chief Shepherd practiced such spiritual disciplines as fasting, prayer and solitude, submission, service, and meditation.[7] If we undershepherds are going to be like our Leader, then we are called into the disciplined life. There can be no denying or escaping this truth. But we must relentlessly stay focused on the goal of the disciplines— Christlikeness. The minute we lose sight of Jesus in our disciplined life, we become legalists, dangerous to ourselves and to others.

This is not a chapter defining the disciplines or the practices of how they are experienced. Dallas Willard, Richard Foster, and John Ortberg are far more competent teachers than I am regarding the vital subject of the spiritual disciplines. Their books are must reading as introductions into the philosophy (Willard) and practice (Foster and Ortberg) of the timeworn, highly effective spiritual disciplines.[8]

This chapter is a plea, a calling for pastors to enter into a life like Christ's, a life that has very clear, transferable behaviors that deeply enrich our personal lives and introduce into our ministries expressions of divine power. Many pastors, coming out of spiritual stagnation, are realizing that, like Jesus, they must make the disciplines a high priority in pastoral ministry. Why?

> *The minute we lose sight of Jesus in our disciplined life, we become legalists, dangerous to ourselves and to others.*

MORE THAN WISHFUL THINKING

The classical spiritual disciplines invite us to participate and grow in actually being like Jesus. First John 2:6 is not just pious wishful thinking. We can live the way Jesus lived in very practical and behavioral ways, becoming like him not only in character (moral transformation), but also in power (ministry transformation). Willard writes: "We *can* become like Christ in character and in power and thus realize our highest ideals of well-being and well-doing. This is the heart of the New Testament message."[9] These two sentences by Willard opened a window for me on a whole new horizon of pastoral ministry.

As I journeyed beyond my introduction into the definitions of and initial attempts at the disciplines (I still have much to learn), I have discovered that the disciplines provide well-defined opportunities to simply love God and be loved by him. The disciplines are actually about intimacy with God. How embarrassed I feel now as I reflect back on my reactions when I first read Foster's practical introduction to the disciplines. I did not have a clue back then (early 1980s) about the powerful and intimate dynamics of a personal and conversational relationship with God.

Dallas Willard presses hard for us to maintain our evangelical integrity when we use terminology like "having a personal relationship with God." In his book *In Search of Guidance*, Willard ably defends the view that God does speak today through means besides the Bible, means that are verified in the Bible but are never in contradiction to the Bible. Believers today, like believers in the Bible, are invited into a "conversational relationship with God." But our evangelical emphasis on "positional truth" may rob believers of individualized, conscious communication from and to God. Willard writes:

> *Sometimes today it seems that our personal relationship to God is spoken of as a mere "arrangement" or "understanding" between Jesus and his Father about us. Our "personal relationship" then only means that each believer has his or her unique "account" in heaven which allows them to draw upon the merits of Christ to pay their sin bills. . . . But who does not think that there should be much more to a* personal relationship *than that?*[10]

I have discovered in the process of practicing the classical spiritual disciplines that they are avenues into greater intimacy with and enjoyment of God. The classical disciplines are considered "classical" because godly saints from the biblical era and on through church history have found them effective means to encounter God in deeply fulfilling and life-changing ways.

I am convinced that a personal encounter with God as Father is the only effective and empowered basis for pastoral ministry. Perhaps our Bible colleges and seminaries *assumed* students were being transformed. I believe that is a faulty and tragic assumption. I heard the stories from my own seminary of men receiving their diplomas (a symbol of good theological knowledge) in one hand and their wives handing them divorce papers (a symbol of some deficiency in the transformation of life) in the other. Without personal, spiritual formation a theological education can be deadly. Not education, not personality, not ability or years of experience can ever replace personal interaction with God as the source of pastoral integrity and authority. The disciplines are doorways into intimate encounters with God. These encounters, which may be stunning at times, will normally and quietly shape and call out our God-designed identity and will position us for God's gracious empowerment for ministry. In solitude and silence a pastor begins to recognize the powerful voice of God. Leanne Payne writes in *Listening Prayer*:

> *What is my vocation? For what purpose was I sent into the world? These may be questions you will want to journal, because* the obedience that comes out of listening to God puts us securely in our truest vocation *(emphasis mine). It is a radical place to be—a place of freedom from the works of the world, the flesh, and the devil. No longer slaves to sin, but alive to God's voice, we are brought into that spacious place of genuine creativity. We are* makers, ourselves made in the image of our Creator God.[11]

We need not have extreme reactions to subjective experiences, reactions that cause us to overlook a distinction that godly men and women have discerned through the ages. This distinction is between the "Word of God" and the "Voice of God." A. W. Tozer clearly states:

> *The Bible is the written word of God, and because it is written it is confined and limited by the necessities of ink and paper and leather. The Voice of God, however, is alive and free as the sovereign God is free. "The words that I speak unto you, they are spirit, and they are life." The life is in the speaking words. God's word in the Bible can have power only because it corresponds to God's word in the universe. It is the Present Voice which makes the written word all-powerful. Otherwise it would be locked in slumber within the covers of a book.[12]*

Because we can learn to listen to God's voice, we can receive pastoral ministry just as Jesus received his ministry. This is a vital observation: *Pastoral ministry is first received before it is achieved.* It was true for Jesus, the Chief Shepherd, and will be so for his undershepherds. Jesus, in defending the radical, nontraditional nature of his ministry, declared, "I tell you the truth, the Son can do nothing by himself; he can do only what he sees the Father doing, because whatever the Father does the Son also does" (John 5:19), and "My teaching is not

> *This is a vital observation: Pastoral ministry is first received before it is achieved.*

my own. It comes from him who sent me" (7:16).

Jesus, as God's appointed agent of salvation, the Messiah, received his ministry, both word and deed, from his heavenly Father. Centuries before Jesus uttered a word, Isaiah prophesied about him receiving his teaching on a daily basis from Yahweh. Isaiah wrote of the Messiah:

> The Sovereign LORD has given me an instructed tongue,
>   to know the word that sustains the weary.
> He wakens me morning by morning,
>   wakens my ear to listen like one being taught.
> The Sovereign LORD has opened my ears
>   and I have not been rebellious;
> I have not drawn back. (Isa. 50:4–5)

Jesus lived in a daily, conversational relationship with God the Father. Salvation introduces us into the wonder of that same kind of relationship. As his part in that relationship, Jesus practiced the spiritual disciplines. As a man, he waited before and listened to the Father. The Father, in turn, did his part, and the Spirit empowered the entire process. Reflecting on the Isaiah 50 passage clarifies like nothing else can why Mark records in his gospel, "Very early in the morning, while it was still dark, Jesus got up, left the house and went off to a solitary place, where he prayed" (Mark 1:35).

Solitude, silence, listening prayer, submission, reception of ministry—those were part of Jesus' daily "walk." If we claim to live in Christ, we must walk as he did. There is no way we will ever become empowered pastors without living the way Jesus did.

The spiritual disciplines rescue the concept of "being like Jesus" from pious hymnody: "Oh, to be like Thee, blessed Redeemer" or "To be like Jesus" or "Lord, I want to be just like you." I grew up singing these great hymns, but I did not have a clue as to any meaningful way to cooperate with the Spirit in actually becoming like Jesus. And outside the church sanctuary, when the singing stopped, Christians who were actually like Jesus in character and power were few and far between.

The disciplines invite us into authentic encounters with the Father, who really does conform us into the image of his Son by the gracious and powerful ministry of the Spirit. In silence and solitude, it is actually possible to hear with our keen inner ears the Spirit testifying with our spirit, "Abba, Father" (Rom. 8:15; Gal. 4:6). We can hear the voice of God saying in clear words audible to our spirit, "You are my son/daughter. With you I am well-pleased." We can engage in a literal conversation with God, Jesus, or the Holy Spirit. What an adventure!

LEARNING THE DISCIPLINES

I was teaching a nine-week course on the disciplines, and for an assignment I directed the class to practice just one hour of strict silence and solitude. When the class reconvened, I asked for their observations about the experience. A number talked about how they discovered that their inner lives were so noisy that it was hard to concentrate. One lady said that she almost gave up, but she persisted until her mind and spirit settled down. Then she said, "God came to me. He spoke so clearly to my spirit, not audibly, yet distinctly, 'You are my treasured daughter. I delight in you. Everything will be all right. I am in control. You are loved.'" By the time she finished telling the class, she had tears in her eyes and a catch in her throat. Several others were getting choked up too. Why? Because we were rejoicing that she met her Father. He came to her personally, lovingly, and authentically. Who wouldn't want that experience?

Knowing that there are yet many pastors like I was—that is, completely uninformed about the disciplines—I would recommend first the process of learning about and imitating two practices of Jesus—solitude and listening prayer. Meditate on Isaiah 50:4–5 and Mark 1:35. These two disciplines are absolutely essential for pastors.

Most pastors are "people persons." They like to be around and relate to people. However, that relational strength can become our crippling weakness. We can easily degenerate from people persons to people pleasers. I know what an ugly and discouraging trap that is. As

Proverbs 29:25 says, "Fear of man will prove to be a snare." The disciplines invite us to experience God as the compelling reality of ministry. And while we will always respect people, we can learn to minister more from the question "What will God think?" than from "What will people think?" The former question is vitally freeing for all believers, especially pastors.

Solitude, silence, Scripture meditation, and listening prayer will readily uncover the subterranean structures of our pastoral ministry as well as of our personal lives. I was shocked to discover in the quiet of God's presence that so much of what I was doing as a pastor had *me* in the center instead of Christ. This kind of discovery can be very agonizing and humbling. Willard explains:

> But solitude, like all the disciplines of the spirit, carries risks. In solitude, we confront our own soul with its obscure forces and conflicts that escape our attention when we are interacting with others. . . . We can only survive solitude if we cling to Christ there. And yet what we find of him in that solitude enables us to return to society as free persons. [13]

Howard Hendricks of Dallas Theological Seminary, a man of God who has profoundly influenced my life, drilled into his students this truth: *If you are always with people, then you will be of no use to people.* Hendricks constantly pointed his students to Christ as the one who knew the value of getting away from people and alone with God.

> *If you are always with people, then you will be of no use to people.*

Regarding solitude, or "the ministry of withdrawal," John Ortberg, a teaching pastor at Willow Creek Community Church in South Barrington, Illinois, writes:

> I need to practice regular withdrawal from ministry. Sometimes it simply involves days off; sometimes it involves a day or a few days of utter solitude. . . . But when I engage in the ministry of withdrawal, I am reminded that I am not indispensable to the church. I am not the messiah. In fact,

*people grow when I am not around in a way they would not if I were
always present.*[14]

Solitude is a paradoxical pastoral practice. In order to be most
effective as pastors to our people, we must leave them so that we can
get alone with the Father. This necessary retreat from people is captured by Eugene Peterson's phrase "the unbusy pastor." Peterson
applies the need for pastoral solitude by citing Herman Melville's
description in *Moby Dick* of the harpooner who rises to his strategic
task. "To insure the greatest efficiency in the dart, the harpooners of
this world must start to their feet out of idleness, and not out of toil."[15]
Solitude, an intentional isolation and purposeful idleness before God,
insures the best efficiency of pastoral work.

Regarding the potential for empowerment, the kind beyond our
wildest imagination, I discovered that there was, for me at least, a def-
inite correlation between cessationist views and loss of intimacy and
power. Cessationist views, with their finely reasoned, systematic arguments about the disappearance of the "sign" gifts, while not intending
to, may end up robbing believers of the very gifts that convey in transforming ways the intimate, powerful love of God.

When Jack Deere, a good friend and competent pastor-theologian,
made the journey from dispensational cessationism to noncessation-
ism, the greatest wonder to him was rediscovering passion for Jesus
and intimacy with God.

> *It took me too long to learn that knowing the Bible is not the same as know-
> ing God, loving the Bible is not the same as loving God, and reading the
> Bible is not the same as hearing God. . . . What I am saying is that it is
> possible to put almost any good thing above Jesus Christ without realiz-
> ing what we are doing. We can put the Bible and its commandments above
> the Lord. We can put the spiritual gifts and even various kinds of worship
> above the Lord. We can put various forms of ministry—witnessing, car-
> ing for the poor, praying for the sick—above the Lord. . . . The essence of
> all of life is loving God and then loving his people (Matthew 22:36–40).*[16]

For all the furor erupting over the topic of spiritual gifts, evangelical noncessationists are really not all that enamored about the recovery and practice of the "sign" gifts as many suppose. While I will
present why I changed my belief to the view that all the gifts are given

and operable in chapter 11, I do not believe that they take center stage. God and his all-embracing love get the spotlight. Because of powerful and deep changes in me, I am much more fascinated by the almighty embrace of a loving Father God.

FREEDOM IN WORSHIP

Since the goal of the disciplines is to foster deepening intimacy with God, an expected consequence of a disciplined life is heartfelt and free worship. God is worthy of our adoration, and worship will become all believers' eternal vocation. As we learn to come near to God through the practice of the disciplines, he truly does come near to us (James 4:8). In the wonder of close communion with God, we respond with adoring submission.

An empowered pastor learns to humble himself or herself before our holy and friendly God and to pour out words of praise and worship. Blessing God and being blessed by him create great momentum to stay true to the grind and glory of pastoring.

> *Blessing God and being blessed by him create great momentum to stay true to the grind and glory of pastoring.*

I remember singing one Sunday morning "Yahweh," a favorite worship song in our church. The song includes these lyrics, "We will worship, we will bow down. . . . We will kneel before the Maker of the universe." As I was singing, the Spirit simply asked me, "Will you, John?"

"Will I what?"

"Will you bow down? Will you kneel before the Maker of the universe?"

"Here, Lord? And now?"

"Yes. Here. Now."

I began to feel that internal press on my spiritual nerve. The "still small voice" was crystal clear. The Master-apprentice training was engaged once again.

I whined, "But what will the people think? They'll think that I'm grandstanding. I don't want to draw attention to me. Besides, people will feel uncomfortable, pressured by my actions, Lord."

"Who are you worshiping, John, the Lord or people? And, really— 'people will feel uncomfortable' or you will feel uncomfortable? Which is it honestly?"

"Okay, Lord. Yes, I am worshiping Yahweh, and, yes, I'm the one feeling uncomfortable about this call to physical expression."

"What do you think your heavenly Father will think if you simply do what the song invites you to do?"

I had entered into another crisis of obedient faith regarding worship. I knew that the chorus was repeated several times, so I still had a chance to obey. The next time the words left my lips, "I will bow down," I went to my knees. Do you know what happened? All the internal arguing and pressure evaporated instantly. I was worshiping as a whole being—mind, spirit, and body. Memories flashed into mind of seeing Muslims bowing low before Allah when I visited Israel, and, in India, Hindus bowing low before images of elephants and monkeys. Is not Yahweh, Maker of heaven and earth, worthy of my bowed adoration? In that surrendered moment, all that mattered was that I was honest and low before my Father, the Creator of all things. My heart was free, and all that seemed important was that I was worshiping my God.

When the song was over and I got up, a part of me wanted to see that the congregation went to its knees too. Yet when I stood I was aware that no one in my section bowed down like me. I did not judge their hearts. I was being urged by the Spirit to search my own. I was free to worship as the Spirit led me. I would give others that freedom as well.

Sometime after this freeing experience in worship, I read some comments by Scotty Smith, pastor of Christ Community Church in Franklin, Tennessee, that greatly encouraged me. In his book *Unveiled Hope*, co-authored by Michael Card, Smith reports an interchange on the freedom of the human body in worship. Smith writes,

> *Another topic of great interest, which generated considerable concern, was whether or not it was appropriate to "lift hands" in public worship. Whole churches were divided over the issue! How sad. I remember a ques-*

tion-and-answer session I attended in seminary, in which Dr. J. I. Packer was asked, "Dr. Packer, what do you think about all of these emotional people coming to our churches and lifting their hands, falling to their knees, and drawing attention to themselves?"

I will never forget his response. "My dear brother," he said with pastoral sensitivity and yet fatherly authority, "the question is not whether we should kneel in our worship services today. The question is, shall we who will kneel one day kneel now as well?" Bingo! That settled the issue for me. Though not mandated, it is appropriate for us to lift our hands, to kneel, to prostrate ourselves, to respond with our whole person to the whole gospel.[17]

I have tried to suggest that empowered pastors, undershepherds like their Chief Shepherd, discover and live out their deepest identity through revelation promise. The Bible defines them and their ministries by bringing God's promises to them. They minister in the supernatural enabling of the Spirit, who still gives all his gifts to the church. They are pastors who engage wandering and broken lives with great "gut-level" compassion just as Jesus engaged people. They are men and women who, through the practice of the spiritual disciplines, enter into intimacy with God and who minister out of that intimacy with the "authority of compassion,"[18] as Henri Nouwen so eloquently puts it. Empowered pastors will lead the church into the next millennium with renewed passion for Christ and received power from the Spirit. This empowered pastoral leadership will recover the role of teaching as they get more acquainted and fall deeper in love with Jesus, the Pastor-Teacher.

JESUS AS PASTOR-TEACHER

THE NATURE OF TEACHING
IN PASTORAL MINISTRY

MY son-in-law, Bryan, loves the sport of rock climbing. He's a rock-climbing fanatic. On the computer on which I am typing this manuscript, Bryan has installed for background wallpaper a breathtaking picture of a tanned and muscular climber scaling the face of a straight wall of rock. Bryan would love to see me in a picture like that, so he has taken me on as his "project."

In Grand Ledge, Michigan, a grand ledge for rock climbing looms right next to the Grand River. Bryan took me there one day. Having learned about carabiners and ropes, harnesses and belaying, I was ready to climb. We secured our webbing at the top of the climbing spot and then hiked down a short trail to the base of the ledge. At the bottom, looking up, I thought, *What's the big deal? This isn't a very high wall. So what's so "grand" about it? This will be a walk in the park. Let's just do it.*

I got into my harness, tied into the ropes, and said to Bryan as I gripped the face of the rock, "Climbing!"

"Climb on," he replied.

I pulled myself up to the first handhold exchange and began to search for the next footholds. I had learned to keep my weight on my legs so that my arms did not have to keep me against the rock. So far, so good. I moved up slowly to the place where I would have to make the next exchanges with my hands and feet. Bryan faithfully belayed, feeding me rope and taking up the slack. *Hey, Mom, look! I'm rock climbing.* Up I went as Bryan yelled directions. I looked down. What? I was a mere five feet from the ground and getting very tired. What looked like such a small ledge a few minutes before now truly looked like a *grand* ledge. I climbed on.

As I got about halfway up the ledge, I encountered a challenging spot for doing the exchanges. I would have to reach up and grip a thin ledge of rock and pull myself up while swinging my right foot to a new hold. Being the agile man that I am, I thought that I could do it as Bryan shouted directions from below. My arms and shoulders ached, but the adrenaline was running. I could do it.

I concentrated on the places my hands and feet would have to go. Then I took a breath and sprang up, reaching and pulling and swinging out my leg. Presto! I was now dangling almost totally upside down. Yes, I was looking down the rock ledge, not up. My center of gravity was in a new orbit and I was strung out awkwardly in space. Somewhere I heard laughing—hearty laughing and words.

"Grab the rock and stop swinging. Get your balance and right yourself."

I thought, *That's easy for you to say.* But clawing and grasping, I did as directed. Soon I was back at the safe place before the fateful leap. After Bryan's laughter subsided, he proceeded with his "project." Me.

"Do it again, but this time get your foot into the hold as you pull yourself up."

I did, and I made it. Then, in a couple of more moves, I was at the top. I had done it. I had conquered Grand Ledge.

TRAINING, NOT TRANSFERRING

Pastoring is a lot more like learning rock climbing than learning something like church history or the argument of the book of Romans. Pastoring is a skill, not a subject.

Jesus Christ defined teaching as training for a way of life, not as transferring information from one mind to another. "A student is not above his teacher, but everyone who is fully trained will be like his teacher" (Luke 6:40). Bryan and his wife, my daughter Elisha, are good rock climbers. They want to train me to be like them. The goal of the teacher, according to Jesus, is to train one's student(s) to be like the teacher. This teaching concept is parallel to God's purpose in our salvation—that is, to make us like his Son (Rom. 8:29). When God is finished with the whole process of our salvation, "we know that when he appears, we shall be like him, for we shall see him as he is" (1 John 3:2).

Earlier I said that preaching provides the revelational landscape in which pastoring is done. I don't personally make a big distinction between preaching and teaching, though many pastors do. Most pastors have heard at least once, "Wow, pastor, today you went from teaching to preaching! God really spoke to me."

Do people intuitively know that real pastoring is bringing God to them, and do they experience that reality in our communication ministry? Do they understand that effective, life-changing communication, whether you call it teaching or preaching, somehow connects them to the living God who is among us? People's hunger for God is real, and they know when that hunger is being met, not with proclaimed truth about God, but by *God himself* through that proclaimed truth.

Preaching and teaching help people discover the places of the heart where they may meet God. As I described earlier, the heart is a vast inner region of being with a geography of its own. Holy Spirit-empowered preaching as a pastoral function points to the map of the soul and invites people to discover God, to make them aware of his presence and his work in their

> *People's hunger for God is real, and they know when that hunger is being met, not with proclaimed truth about God, but by God himself through that proclaimed truth.*

lives. Empowered preaching declares with Isaiah, "Here is your God!" (Isa. 40: 9).

Most people and, sadly, many pastors have lost connection with the whole universe of the inner life. This is symptomatic of our Western culture. Leonard Sweet observes, "In a day when our intellectual and technological intelligence is skyrocketing, . . . our emotional and spiritual intelligence is flat. . . . The modern world sucked the soul out of life."[1] Our souls have been flattened by materialism and consumerism. Against the broader backdrop of an atheistic evolutionary theory of human origins, the rich landscape of our inner lives has been horribly eroded. But things are changing and bringing us back to the wonder of discovering our souls. Jesus' words once again invite investigation.

Jesus likens our hearts to differing types of soil (Mark 4:1–20) and speaks of our innermost being flowing with rivers of water (John 7:37–39). The Bible's use of geographical imagery to describe our lives invites us to imagine ourselves as panting deer being chased through the forests (Ps. 42:1–2), as deep waters (Prov. 20:5) or muddied springs and polluted wells (Prov. 25:26), as a dark and crooked maze that no one but God can comprehend (Jer. 17:9–10), as a tenderly cared-for vineyard (Isa. 5:1–7; see also John 15:1–8), as wheat or weeds in fertile farmland (Matt. 13:37–43), and as fish in the sea (Matt. 13:47–50). All these images and more intend to draw us back to the rich and varied landscape of the soul and to invite us to meet God at various places there. My heart isn't just Christ's home; it's his universe.

Teaching and preaching help people read the maps of their inner lives. A challenging rock to climb will be mapped, showing its several routes. The routes, like ski slopes on a Colorado mountain, are categorized according to degree of difficulty. As you know the degree of difficulty, you can weigh that against your level of skill and experience. Preaching and teaching define the maps; pastoring engages people in their particular challenges, calling out the directions, encouragments, and warnings as they climb on.

Or, to change the metaphor, just as in any exciting trip, the thrill is not in getting to know the map. This seems to be the primary goal of much evangelical teaching, with the map being the Bible. An exciting trip means more than reading the map; it means enjoying the sights and sounds of the places along the way. For the Christian, the destination is always God, and who will ever be able to fully explore him?

GOD AMONG THE PEOPLE

Jesus was known as a Teacher,[2] but he was a Pastor-Teacher. His incarnate purpose was to bring God to people. In fact, he was God among the people! And while among us, he taught. The Gospels pulsate with his voice teaching the people in a variety of ways and in a variety of settings. His teaching was aimed at the "heart," the epicenter of the soul, for he knew that the Father's purpose, grounded in new covenant promise, was to give people a "new heart." Only changed hearts will lead to changed behaviors. The religious leaders, so hostile to Jesus, were masters at "behavior modification," but their hearts were far from God (see Mark 7:6–8).

Jesus commissioned his disciples with both authority and a mandate to teach (Matt. 28:18–20). In particular, Jesus commissioned Peter to pastor his (Jesus') sheep by feeding them. That "feeding" began with Peter taking the lead to *apply Scripture* to Judas Iscariot's death and replacement (Acts 1), and powerfully to *apply Scripture* as a witness of Christ's resurrection and exaltation and the subsequent outpouring of the Holy Spirit (Acts 2). Peter became a Spirit-empowered communicator who brought God to people in the rocky terrain of their hearts (Acts 2:37: "cut to the heart"). The early church "devoted themselves to the apostles' teaching" (Acts 2:42), and teaching still has a primary place in the life of the church.

The empowered pastor will teach, but his or her goal is to teach for transformed lives that have the living Christ as focus, pattern, and destination. Of course, there is much content to convey, so I'm not trying to play the heart against the mind. I had to learn about harnesses, ropes, and specialized gear for rock climbers as I began the sport with Bryan. But getting to the rock and *climbing* was the goal of the learning. Getting the Bible content across to others is simply a step toward the ultimate goal—*to see Christ actually formed in and living through people.* Paul labored hard as a communicator, both in person and through writing, to achieve this purpose. He wrote, "My dear children, . . . I am again in the pains of childbirth until Christ is formed in you" (Gal. 4:19).

Paul provides an intriguing analysis of his teaching method in 1 Corinthians 2:1–5. He defines his content in verse 2: "I resolved to know nothing while I was with you except Jesus Christ and him crucified." Paul confesses in this verse the two essential features of his teaching content: (1) the person of Christ, and (2) the redeeming work of Christ. That is the revelatory content of his message. Yet it is fascinating to see how Paul concludes this declaration to the Corinthians. Verse 5 does not end with "so that your faith might not rest on men's wisdom, but on God's *truth*," that is, the content of the person and work of Christ. Rather, Paul startlingly ends his thought with "but on God's *power*." The operative presence of God meeting and changing the Corinthians is the place where their faith must rest.

Paul knew the strategic role of revelatory content, to provide a location for people to be met and changed by the powerful God. A few verses later Paul says, "The kingdom of God is not a matter of talk but of power" (1 Cor. 4:20). Even when that talk is full of divine content, lives are not changed if there is no expression of the operative power of God. We need both the truth and the Spirit for the transformational purpose of pastor-teaching to occur.

In the fascinating story about his life and ministry, Jim Cymbala writes in *Fresh Wind, Fresh Fire:*

> Let me make a bold statement: Christianity is not predominantly a teaching religion. We have been almost overrun by the cult of the speaker.... It is fine to explain about God, but far too few people today are experiencing the living Christ in their lives. We are not seeing God's visitation in our gatherings. We are not on the lookout for his outstretched hand.
>
> The teaching of sound doctrine is a prelude, if you will, to the supernatural.[3]

This is an extremely bold and necessary word for today's American evangelical church. Cymbala's courage is commendable, and he writes with a passionate pastor's heart.

MAKING SENSE

Our teaching has to make sense to the people we serve. It must touch their lives. "Jesus' followers were drawn to him largely because his teaching made so much sense.... They discovered they could trust him as their teacher."[4]

When I was in the Ukraine, a pivotal pastor-teaching moment presented itself in an unusual way. In the Ukraine the tensions between "charismatic" and "noncharismatic" views are sadly as evident as in the United States. During the course of my teaching on spiritual nurture and discipleship, my students asked me to teach them some songs we sing in the United States.

One song I selected was the older tune called "Spirit of the Living God." I learned this song in my student years at Moody Bible Institute, and I had never sung it with any sense that it was controversial. Well, welcome to Ukraine! I got word that my teaching that song was "out of bounds" with the prevailing noncharismatic wing of the church. Apparently the phrase where we sing to the Spirit, "Fall afresh on me," went too far for some holding to noncharismatic Ukrainian theology.

I was told that *because* "charismatics" sing that song in their churches, we could not sing that song in class. While I did not understand or agree with the logic forbidding the song, I did not want to purposely offend the church leaders, so I ceased having the class sing "Spirit of the Living God."

My purpose in telling this story is in no way to disparage Ukrainian views about the Spirit, but to pinpoint the need for bold pastor-teaching. As a pastor-teacher I wrestled with what was being communicated to the students in this whole issue. That we could not sing a song because another group sang it did not make sense. Where would that kind of thinking end? I decided to take a risk.

After the decision to cease singing the song, I went into class the next morning and asked some questions of my students. Ukraine has a delicious soup called *borscht*. I could eat that soup every day at every meal. The Ukrainian students enjoy it too. I asked the students, "Do charismatics eat *borscht?*"

"Yes," they answered.

"Then we shall not eat *borscht* because we do not want to be viewed as charismatics." I asked another question: "Do charismatics read the Bible in Ukraine?"

"Yes," they said.

"Then we shall not read the Bible, for we might be viewed as charismatics." I pressed on. "Do charismatics pray in Ukraine?"

"Yes," they replied.

"Then we shall not pray, for we might be considered charismatics."

By now the students were beginning to see the point. That we could not sing a simple prayer to the Spirit just because another differing group sang it was very faulty reasoning. That would trap us in the tiniest world of all—not being able to do anything "they" do.

As far as I know there is nothing about the song "Spirit of the Living God" that is essentially charismatic or noncharismatic. Here's the irony in this story. I told the students that on the previous Sunday night I had been in the church of the pastor who had the biggest concern over our classes singing "Spirit of the Living God." His choir sang—are you ready for this?—"Majesty." The song "Majesty," a wonderful song about Jesus Christ, was penned by a Pentecostal pastor and well-respected Christian leader, Jack Hayford. Why could the church choir sing a song that charismatics sing?

My students mulled over our class discussion for a few days. They knew I cared about them and wanted them to learn to think biblically. So later they came to class and said, "Mr. Frye, we want to eat *borscht*. We want to sing 'Spirit of the Living God.' Will you lead us?"

As a pastor-teacher I was gratified. I knew that they had thought through the faulty reasoning of why the song had been pulled. Petty issues must not divert us from the major issues of encountering God and becoming like Jesus. I was able now to lead them into why it would still not be wise to sing it. I did not want to foster even a hint of a spirit of rebellion against their church leadership. I wanted much more to shape their hearts and minds with the Spirit of Jesus than to defend or define what songs they should sing.

TELLING THE TRUTH

> *Pastor-teaching becomes truly effective when revealed truth is honestly communicated from a life that is under constant transformation.*

One final reality has dawned on me regarding teaching. Pastor-teaching becomes truly effective when revealed truth is honestly communicated from a life that is under constant transformation. When I tell how a truth is convicting me, shaping me, giving me hope, giving me direction, then I most likely will hear people say, "John, God really spoke to me today through the message."

I don't know why it has taken me so long to see that pastoral leadership (through the teaching gift) is really all about life change—in me as well as in my congregation. Pastors are not only to exegete the Word, but their lives as well. Did not Paul teach the concept that we believers are letters read by others (2 Cor. 3:1–3)?

One of the most well-received series of messages at Bella Vista Church (where I have served for seventeen years now) was one I preached in 1989 called "Finding the Father." In that series my aim was to connect people to God as their heavenly Father. Not only did I work with the biblical texts that reveal what God the Father means to us, I also told most of my own story. I opened up my life and spoke of my own fatherlessness and my personal quest (and need) to find God as my Father. By the grace of God, many lives in the church were deeply touched and profoundly changed.

In the combination of exegeted Scripture and expressed personal need, God met people in authentically transforming ways. A phrase from that old hymn celebrating the gift of Scripture took on life: "Beyond the sacred page, we seek you, Lord." In recent years I "dusted off" and reworked that series calling it "Enjoying God as Father." This series, too, had a life-changing impact on many. Being a spiritual leader means revealing how God is leading me and then inviting people to follow.

> The world does not need to see a lot of people devoted to Christ. They need to see Jesus himself.

The world does not need to see a lot of people devoted to Christ. They need to see Jesus himself. People are coming to our churches to meet God, not to hear about God. Let's bring God to them.

JESUS AND SPIRITUAL CONFLICT

THE CONTEXT OF THE PASTORAL CALLING

"AVOID conflict" was my middle name. I was the pastorally "nice guy" who swept through the church like the old vaudevillian crying, "Is evvvverrrrybody haaaap-PY?" I thought I was a real peacemaker. What I really was, however, was a pain-avoider. While pain-avoiders may look like peacemakers, there is a world of difference between the two.

I would often hear, "John, you don't like confrontation, do you?" While I would smile politely on the outside and mumble something like "You're right, that isn't my personality (or gift or temperament or style, *ad infinitum*)," on the inside I would knot up thinking, "No! A thousand times, no! I hate confrontation!" I wanted everybody to be at peace, to be happy. I was under the delusion of and congratulating myself for being a fine "peacemaker."

When I sought counseling for the alarming emergence of my deep, dark side, I was skillfully led to the painful realization that my alleged peacemaking efforts were not all that commendable. The naked truth came out—I was not a peacemaker; I was a pain-avoider. By powerfully suppressing my childhood traumas of "abandonment and engulfment,"[1] I made it my mission in life to avoid pain of any kind. People in conflict or unhappy around me, heated arguments and threats, and divisions and factions caused the tip of a massive iceberg of pain (my own deep pain) to surface. Driven by my inner compulsions at "peacemaking," I worked like a madman to push that iceberg of pain-turned-rage back down so it could stay buried and forgotten. I appeared to others as a "peacemaker," yet in reality, because of my own inner brokenness and bondage, I was actually a cowardly pain-avoider.

I came to learn a basic Christian reality: "Our struggle is not against flesh and blood . . . but against the powers of this dark world" (Eph. 6:12). My Enemy (and yours) relentlessly exploited every dimension of brokenness and trauma in my life. Lurking in the submerged regions of my inner life were "powers of this dark world" using my persisting denial, frantic peacemaking, and panicked flight from my past to keep me in bondage.

I am not saying that I was "demon-possessed" and that my counselor had to "exorcise" wicked spirits from me. As a matter of fact, the topic of spiritual warfare never became an issue for us. In the process of healing, I surprisingly discovered the amazing correlation between my personal "flesh and blood" history and the mission of the "powers of this dark world" to destroy me. In the process of recovery, I had to reclaim my given middle name, ironically the name of my father, "Wallace." My false, self-constructed middle name, "Avoid Conflict," uttered by my functional denial, had to go.

Conflict is a spiritual reality and has been since Lucifer rebelled against God (see Isa. 14 and Ezek. 28 if you believe that behind the human agents described in these chapters there is also a reference to Satan). Since the serpent tempted Eve and she and Adam sinned in Eden, friction has defined relationships. Conflict is the outworking of the divine curse of "enmity" between the seed of the woman and the seed of the serpent (Gen. 3:15).

Where two or three are gathered together, there you have problems. Human conflict, the battle of the wills, is inevitable in a fallen world, and the local church is not immune. As some pastors read this statement about conflict, they are all too well aware of the pain that it brings—to them, their families, their friends. Pastorally I used to hydroplane over the surface of conflicts, seeking to patch things up, while ignorant of and unskilled in pastoring in the realm of the Spirit and spirits where *the real conflicts lie.*

WRESTLING ONE ON ONE

I am captivated by Paul's use of the verb "wrestle" in Ephesians 6:12 (KJV). It is a *bapaxlogomena*—a fancy word meaning that Paul used this term only once in his writings. As one observes the passage, "wrestle" seems at first awkward and gangly, like it doesn't fit. Paul continues in Ephesians 6 to define the armor of God that we Christian soldiers must put on to fight. But wait—wrestlers don't wear armor. Wrestlers don't do contest in regiments or battalions. A wrestling match in Paul's day, even as in our own, was one on one. How well I know.

As a student at Moody Bible Institute, I was on the wrestling team. While on a "team," the actual wrestling match was not a team event. I had to face my opponent alone. The team could cheer or groan with me, but it was against the rules for another team member to jump in and help me take down my opponent. What is my point?

In living out the Christian life, we do not *wrestle* against human beings; we wrestle against a fierce Enemy and his destructive, wicked powers. An actual and deadly active spiritual realm exists. Pastoral ministry accepts and engages this realm as the playing field on which to do pastoral work. Pastors must make clear to each child of God, each member on the team, the individual nature of spiritual warfare— that is, the real and deadly conflict, and equip and coach each individual believer in skills to win the match.

> *Pastors must make clear to each child of God, each member on the team, the individual nature of spiritual warfare.*

I thank God for Christian leaders like Dr. C. Fred Dickason,[2] a man and theologian whom I highly respect. I do so because he, through his teaching when I was a first-year student at Moody, introduced me in his "Theology Proper" class to the awesome, sovereign attributes of the God we love and serve. Dr. Dickason takes spiritual warfare seriously and seeks to equip believers to win the match against evil beings who threaten their lives.

Other leaders as well realize that much of the downfall of the evangelical church does not stem from a lack of expository preaching. While many continue to shout, "We need more, more, more good biblical preaching," others recognize that the church's demise stems in large measure from a lack of serious, practical equipping in the skills of spiritual warfare. To correct this, many evangelical leaders are writing and conducting seminars. Books by leaders such as Timothy Warner,[3] Neil Anderson,[4] Clinton Arnold,[5] and the late pastor D. Martyn Lloyd-Jones[6] give excellent training for the individual contests we all face with the Enemy. Another Christian leader who has helped me and the church I pastor is Dr. Victor M. Matthews.

In early 1995 Dr. Matthews conducted a ten-week Wednesday night Bible class in our church called "Spiritual Warfare and the Christian Life." What an incredible series this was for many of us in particular and for our church in general. One of Matthews's most liberating points was that behind every act of sin there is a received lie from the Enemy. Forgiveness through the blood of Jesus Christ deals with our *acts* of sin as we agree with God about, or confess, those acts. Spiritual warfare is defined simply as living in the realm of total reality as revealed in the Scripture that requires engaging hostile spiritual beings. We must resist the Enemy and his lies that provoke our acts of sin. Through careful biblical development, Dr. Matthews led us deeper into Christian reality as we were equipped without fear to engage the lies lodged deeply in our spirits by Satan, the Father of Lies. These lies are intended to defeat, discourage, and if possible to destroy us.

I have a friend who is the director of a Christian ministry in our city. The board of this ministry will not adopt a strong doctrinal statement regarding Satan and warfare. Why? Because in their thinking, to discuss Satan or to be precise about him "glorifies" him and gives him freedom to function. They think avoidance is the best way to deal with Satan and warfare issues. I cannot imagine how diabolically pleased the Enemy is with this kind of "head in the sand" approach to him and his wily schemes. "Ignorance is bliss" is bliss only for the Enemy's side!

Dr. D. Martyn Lloyd-Jones lamented that warfare issues are missing from most of our discussions of Christian growth. "Much teaching concerning holiness and sanctification never even mentions the devil and these dark powers at all. The problem is regarded solely as something confined to us. Hence the total inadequacy of many proposed solutions."[7] All the statistical data about the moral compromises of the evangelical church scream out for solutions. Spirit-empowered pastors who follow Jesus Christ will look through what is seen to what is unseen and engage the Enemy and his evil works. Pastors will also equip others to do so.

TAKING THE DEVIL SERIOUSLY

Neil Anderson and Charles Mylander write in their book, *Setting Your Church Free*, that pastors are targets of the Enemy. "Pastors sense a spiritual struggle is going on and discern that they themselves are the target of the archenemy. Unexplained hassles, marriage pressures, physical illness, conflicts with close associates and feelings of inadequacy often plague pastors. What is scary is that these defy rational explanation, occurring far too often and for no apparent reason."[8] Pastors must take spiritual warfare seriously.

Since this is a book about Jesus as the Senior Pastor, we are right in asking, "What place did Jesus give to Satan and warfare issues in his ministry?" We must ask whether or not Jesus took Satan and demons seriously and whether he equipped his followers to engage the Enemy in the realm of spirits.

A cursory reading of the Gospels stuns us with the reality of the engagement Jesus initiated against his (and our) personal Enemy, Satan, and other evil beings called demons. Soon after his baptism by John in the Jordan when Jesus received the anointing of the Spirit for his vocation as Messiah, Jesus was compelled (literally "thrown") by the Spirit into the wilderness, where he wrestled one on one with Satan himself. As the Second Adam, Jesus was tempted to violate the will of God as the first Adam had done. Yet unlike the first Adam, Jesus, with the sword of the Spirit, the Word (*rhema*) of God, repeatedly defeated the Enemy (see Matt. 4; Luke 4).

In episodes of spiritual battle too numerous to report here, Jesus engaged and cast out demons whose sole mission is to destroy human life. The classic case is the exorcism of a "legion" of demons from the tormented man of the Gadarenes (see Mark 5:1–20). In missiological terms this text describes what is known as a "power encounter."

Jesus confronted and defeated with his Word an army ("legion") of destroying demons. This happened in time and space on the rocky cliffs near the northeastern corner of the Galilean seaside. With his authority and his Word, Jesus liberated a man whose sole and ultimate cause for fierce demonic attack was that he as a human being bore "the image of God."

Satan hates human beings because they are made in and bear God's image. Satan hates us because he so fiercely hates God. According to William Lane's provoking observation about the contest between Jesus and the "Legion" of the Gadarenes, Satan will lie, deceive, tempt, accuse, steal, attack, and scheme in order to achieve one diabolical plan: to bring death to people.[9]

When I consider those within the evangelical church who think that avoiding thoughts and discussion about Satan, demons, and warfare is the best approach to these topics, I wonder what they do with the Lord's Prayer. In that model prayer Jesus bluntly teaches us to pray, "Lead us not into temptation, but deliver us from the evil one" (Matt. 6:13). With this one phrase Jesus himself opens the window for us to the battlefield where spiritual warfare takes place. How can we as Christian pastors, through this prayer, affirm our celebration of the Father in worship, invoke his kingdom and will, receive and offer forgiveness, ask and receive our daily needs, and then blatantly believe that we can ignore the Enemy and spiritual warfare without detrimental consequences? It does not make sense!

Not only did our Senior Pastor engage in warfare and teach his followers to pray about warfare, he even equipped others for spiritual warfare. When Jesus sent out the Twelve, he gave them heavenly authority to drive out evil spirits (Matt. 10:1). Later, when not just the Twelve, but the seventy-two who were sent out by Jesus returned, they excitedly and joyfully reported, "Lord, even the demons submit to us in your name" (Luke 10:17). Luke sets the sending out of the seventy-two in the context of the harvest ready to be reaped. People, like whitened fields, are prepared for harvest. An aspect of harvesting is engaging in spiritual warfare.

Jesus, the Senior Pastor, imparts to his undershepherds a spiritual authority that enables them to powerfully, effectively, and victoriously engage the Enemy and his wicked hosts without fear. Without fear does not mean without respect for the fierce opponents that Satan and his legions are; but with "the Name" we are equipped to do spiritual battle. When we speak the name of Jesus Christ, the whole universe comes to attention.

> Jesus ... imparts to his undershepherds a spiritual authority that enables them to powerfully, effectively, and victoriously engage the Enemy and his wicked hosts without fear.

The supernatural gifts of the Spirit (see again 1 Cor. 12:7–11) equip the church for warfare in the realm of spirits. A correlation can be made between the gifts of "distinguishing between spirits" and "miraculous powers" and the church's responsibility and authority to "resist the devil and he will flee from you." The church is commanded and empowered to engage in spiritual warfare and to do so effectively.

While actual exorcisms are rare, confronting satanic lies is a common and ongoing aspect of spiritual war.[10] As a pastor I was ill equipped to understand my own bondages, much less the bondages of others. While I don't totally "blame" Satan, I now readily acknowledge that Satan deviously exploited my spirit with all its wounds.

Satan had staked out a large segment of emotional and spiritual real estate in me. He tricked me into believing I was a peacemaker when I was clearly a pain-avoider. He caused me through denial to shield my broken heart from God's healing grace. He led me to believe that running from pain was being like Jesus. How wrong! Jesus is described as "a man of sorrows, and familiar with suffering" (Isa. 53:3). I feared ever being described like that. I wanted myself and others to be removed from sorrow and suffering. How wrong, immature, and destructive!

People must not only *hear* the gospel; they must *experience* it as Jesus the anointed deliverer offers to them an awesome inner liberation—what the Bible calls "salvation." Jesus alone "breaks the power of canceled sin; he sets the prisoners free"!

A LIBERATING POWER

I wrote earlier about attending Leanne Payne's Pastoral Ministry School on the Wheaton College campus. As I said, Leanne, an evangelical in the Episcopal church, has been called to address with the gospel of Jesus Christ those who are held in the horrible bondage of sexual addictions. These sessions at the Billy Graham Center involved a time of worship followed by intriguing Bible-based lectures and finally a time of ministry where the Holy Spirit was invited to come. The Spirit did come, bringing the liberating power of the gospel to those trapped in sexual sins. I saw and heard the dark, destructive powers as the Spirit of the exalted Christ engaged them. Those unclean spirits, just as it is recorded in the Gospels, caused loud shrieking in some, yet those same unclean spirits obediently fled as Jesus' name was invoked and applied.

The deliverance ministry was startling and unsettling. I saw before my eyes and I heard with my ears the living reality of Luke 4:18–19 activated by the Spirit of God. While people were being delivered, those of us who were literally *observing* the gospel were led in singing Martin Luther's "A Mighty Fortress Is Our God." I will never be able to sing that great hymn again without seeing and hearing the tremendously powerful liberation that Jesus, the present Savior, was bringing to those held in sexual bondage.

> And though this world with devils filled,
>   should threaten to undo us,
> we will not fear, for God hath willed
>   his truth to triumph through us.
> . . . the Spirit and the gifts are ours,
>   through him who with us sideth.

Some good friends, Dr. Steve and Judy King, were at the Leanne Payne conference as well. Dr. King is a psychiatrist, and Judy is a clinical social worker. Both are competently trained and have years of experience in both psychological and spiritual service. I trust them.

At the break I asked Steve to help me interpret what went on in the very dramatic, if not traumatic, service. I was a little excited— unnerved actually. I told Steve that I had never seen anything like it and that I had a question.

"How do you, Steve, as a Christian psychiatrist process all that you are seeing and hearing? How do you explain it?"

"John, I see it often in my office as a psychiatrist. When people get in touch with deep pain and bondage, they will cry out, groan, even collapse. But it's usually just one on one. What you have witnessed is the Holy Spirit, the divine Counselor, bringing freedom and healing in a corporate setting. What I often see privately in my office, you are seeing openly in this ministry of healing. It's simply the Holy Spirit powerfully applying the redeeming work of Jesus to these very needy lives."

"Oh," I said.

I felt a sense of relief. Steve's explanation rang true. Why would anyone limit the mighty Spirit of God from doing such a gracious, if not raucous, work?

Empowered pastors accept spiritual conflict as a way of life. They

Empowered pastors accept spiritual conflict as a way of life.

are not just dealing with the inevitable "flesh and blood" skirmishes; they are using biblical and Spirit-empowered insight to engage in spiritual battles. They are going behind the scenes (as we see in the book of Job) and taking on the devil and his hosts. By entering into warfare this way,[11] we too will be like Jesus, the Senior Pastor.

COLLABORATORS WITH JESUS

BRINGING GOD'S PERCEPTIBLE PRESENCE

OUR church's executive pastor and I were attending a seminar on worship and men's ministry led by Jack Hayford. The seminar was held in a beautiful and very large conference room in an East Coast city. Rows of chairs, tightly squeezed together, seemed as long as the Nile. Because I am involved in both the worship and men's ministries of our church, I was primed and ready to learn all I could.

In the evening session, during Jack's teaching presentation, he suddenly stopped midsentence, which seemed quite unusual to me. After a pause, he said, "I sense the Lord Jesus is here, wanting to pass by many of you. He wants to pass by as he did blind Bartimaeus, who was calling out to Christ, 'Son of David, have mercy on me!' Remember what Jesus asked Bartimaeus? Jesus asked, 'What do you want me to do for you?' Friends, Jesus is here now, walking by us, and he's asking the same question, 'What do you want me to do for you?' Let's go to our knees as Jesus walks by us."

I was surprised and, I admit, a little skeptical. *How does he know Jesus is here, passing by each one of us?* I wondered. Yet I was also deeply expectant, my heart longing for Jesus to pass by me. I went to my knees, cramped in between the rows of chairs along with many hundreds of others.

Jesus did pass by me. I was aware of his real and inquiring presence. In my spirit I heard him ask me, "John, what do you want me to do for you?" My heart welled up with longings, and I silently poured them out to Jesus. He was *present*. I began to cry quietly, for it seemed Jesus was in front of me listening and caring.

I'm a little embarrassed to admit it, but I was so enthralled by Jesus' visit that I didn't hear Jack resume teaching. When I opened my eyes and looked up, everybody was back in their chairs facing Jack and listening, and I was still down on my knees facing away from Jack. How could I get up without being noticed? I was feeling thrilled and silly all at the same time.

Jack Hayford is a pastor and teacher who has learned to be aware of the perceptible presence of Jesus Christ. God wanted not so much for me to learn more about worship and men's ministry at that conference, but to experience that evening encounter with the perceptibly present Christ. Jesus began and is still doing those things I asked when I poured out my heart to him that night.

A CARING WORD

About two years after that encounter with Jesus, I was with some friends who had attended the Leanne Payne conference on healing prayer. This group of friends meets periodically to encourage and pray for one another. On this particular occasion the group prayed for me, and Jesus met me again, but in a very different way.

Our practice is to gather around the one who is to be prayed for, lay hands on him or her, seek the Lord for direction in prayer, and then pray. They had gathered around me, and two good friends began praying. One man is a laid-back, gentle-spirited person who is a respected psychiatrist. The other is a licensed psychologist and seminar leader. During this time of prayer I became the recipient of a prophetic word of knowledge. This caring, prophetic word brought the impact of Christ's perceptible presence in a different way than Christ's perceptible presence under Jack Hayford's ministry.

Here is how it took place. The group was praying, and I heard one of the couples softly praying in spiritual languages ("tongues"). The others were asking the Lord for guidance in English. I was asking the Lord to hear and answer all our prayers. I wanted to receive from Jesus what he had for me. Then one of the women spoke to me with laser-accurate insight even though I had never had a discussion with her about my past. She spoke, "John, I think the Lord is giving me a picture. I see a little boy about ten years old. He is very frightened, feeling very alone and in the dark. He is crying. I see this, John. Does it mean anything to you?"

Instantly, a powerful visual replay was displayed on the screen of my mind. I was ten years old, living in the navy housing complex in Key West, Florida, and it was sundown. My mother, working second shift at a hotel gift shop, was gone, and my father, working on the navy base, was supposed to come home and be with me. My father never showed. (He was out with a married woman committing adultery.) So there I was—alone. My friends had all gone home for supper. It was getting dark, and I was afraid to go into the dark apartment by myself. I was sitting on the lid of the metal trash can at the end of the sidewalk, crying into the darkening night, "Mommy, where are you? Daddy, where are you?"

Abandoned. Feeling so abandoned. Imagine the terrified agony of that little ten-year-old boy. It all came back to me in a flood of feeling triggered by my friend's prophetic revelation. I told the group what I was seeing and feeling. Under the loving prayers of my good friends, I began to cry. Dr. Matthews prayed, "Lord Jesus, show John, show that little boy, that though he felt the strong fear of his father and mother forsaking him, you, Jesus, never did. Show John that you were there with him, loving him."

Immediately I had a memory of our family's coffee table Bible. That Bible seemed as big as Noah's ark and was more for public display than for personal reading. As chaotic as my parents' marriage was, in our navy apartment we not only had the destructive dysfunction of an alcoholic man, we had that huge coffee table Bible. On the cover of that Bible was a reproduction of Solomon's *Head of Christ*. The Lord Jesus met me in those prayers through the memory of that picture of Christ, reassuring me that he, indeed, had been with me, that he had never left me.

I cried some more. Deeply lodged feelings of abandonment that the devil had used against me were taken out of his diabolical arsenal. The present Christ brought deeply meaningful healing to some long-forgotten memories buried in the strata of my soul.

Why am I telling you this? Jesus Christ wants to make his presence perceptible, known in experience. He will manifest himself in ways that affirm that he is Immanuel, God with us. These periodic perceptible visitations are meant to encourage, comfort, and bring hope and healing. Christ's manifested presence at the Hayford seminar brought hope and expectancy about my future as a person and as a pastor. Christ's perceptible presence through my friends' ministry of prayer brought healing from sin-wreckage in my past.

> *Jesus Christ wants to make his presence perceptible, known in experience. He will manifest himself in ways that affirm that he is Immanuel, God with us.*

These perceptible visitations do not threaten the truth that we are to live by faith and not by sight. They bolster faith and serve to get us through the times when we do live by raw faith alone—through what Saint John of the Cross termed "the dark night of the soul." God is a person, and like any person, he can be experienced. In fact, God longs to be experienced. "Now this is eternal life: that they may know you, the only true God, and Jesus Christ, whom you have sent" (John 17:3).

MORE THAN TELLING

Elementary Bible students soon learn that the verb *know* is more powerful and profound than *know about*. It is the verb of intimate, personal knowledge. Eternal life is experiential intimacy with God and his Son, Jesus Christ. An Old Testament usage of the verb can be found in Genesis 4:1: "Adam knew Eve his wife; and she conceived" (KJV). *Knowing about* does not produce babies.

Pastors can easily succumb to the distortion that it is our job to make God known by merely talking about him. We have to tell about God, tell about his presence, tell about his attributes, tell about his will, and tell about his coming. Tell, tell, tell. People are conditioned to believe that knowing God's presence is equal to their simply affirming what the pastor or teacher tells.

Pastoral ministry is not just telling about God's presence. Pastoring is about learning to pray for, detect, and bring God's presence. "For the kingdom of God is not a matter of talk but of power" (1 Cor. 4:20). As we listen with grace-sensitive ears and watch with God-curious eyes, we will be able to read the presence of God in the stories of other people's lives. This can happen one on one with a person, in small groups, in times of corporate worship, and during preaching. What is so amazing is that God really does show up. He manifests—makes visible—his omnipresence. At times, as we seek him daily in faith and obedience, he comes perceptibly. And when he does, we are never the same.

We are to live by faith and not by these perceptions of God's real presence, but we are not to rule out the reality of and need for these God visitations either. I am learning, as Saint Augustine wrote about long ago in his *Confessions*, that we have been built with inner spiritual components that correspond to our physical senses.[1] We have "eyes of the heart" that can be enlightened, we have "ears" that can hear what the Spirit says, and we have "arms" that can embrace the truth and the Savior (the Greek word for "receive" is built on the concept "to warmly embrace"). We have "inward parts" that can feel and impart the compassion of God. We have a spiritual "mind" that can be darkened or can receive "the mind of Christ." We have an "inner person," an entire region of being existing in the realm of spirit that is designed to apprehend the very presence of God.

Why are we built this way? We are made with the capacity to be aware of and enjoy the perceptible presence of God. These spiritual organs are activated by faith, but once activated, look out, for the adventure begins! The pastoral adventure is to make the inner person strong, alert, and experienced in God-sightings. As pastors grow in their own ability to perceive God's presence, they become capable, as priests of God, to perceive and report God's presence to others.

I used to be encouraged when, after a Sunday's message, people would say, "John, that was a good message. You showed me things from that verse that I never would have seen. I don't know how you do it. Thanks so much." Howard Hendricks called this postservice time "the glorification of the worm." (Good stuff, eh?) People still say similar things to me, but I have noticed something about the postmessage comments that brings a greater sense of encouragement. Now I often hear, "John, the Lord met me today through the message. He was talking right to me." Or, "John, during the prayer time, God came right by me and spoke to me about some things in my life." Or, "During our worship singing, the Spirit met me and broke me. He loved

me and gave me new hope." These are God-sightings, God's perceptible presence.

Didn't the apostle John have a revelation of the exalted Christ
walking among the lampstands? Doesn't John go on to say that the
lampstands are local, geographically pinpointed churches—the seven
churches of Asia Minor (see Rev. 1–3)? Isn't it a valid applicational
reality that the exalted Christ still "walks" among his local churches,
not only in Asia Minor, but also in West Michigan, where my church
is located, and in your town or city too?

The apostle John was "in the Spirit," while in prayer. John was in
solitude (forced due to exile on Patmos) and was worshiping (it was
the Lord's Day). It was then that John had a God-sighting of cosmic
proportions. He perceived the presence of Christ both for himself and
for others, and he reported it.

A MINISTRY OF TEARS

Remember my friend Kurt Dillinger, whom I wrote about in an earlier chapter? One Sunday evening we were conducting what we call
the "Ministry of Hope." It is a monthly service in which the elders and
other trained prayer ministers are available to pray for the needs of
the people who come. We pray for all kinds of needs with all kinds
of prayers. We pray for healing—physical (with anointing with oil),
emotional, spiritual, and relational. Kurt was there as part of the
prayer team.

A woman came whom Kurt knew well. He was aware of much of
the pain in her past. After this woman expressed her immediate, presenting need, we gathered around her and began to pray. Soon we
heard a man crying softly. The cries became louder and turned into
sobs. Agonizing cries. We were all a little surprised by this. It was
Kurt. He didn't pray. He cried.

Later we asked Kurt what happened. He said that a deep compassion came over him for the woman. He said the cries welled up in him
and came from somewhere beyond him. Kurt was feeling the heart of
Jesus, our sympathetic High Priest, for the pain carried in the life of
this woman. Kurt was a little embarrassed by the cries but believed
that he was simply making real and visible and audible how God felt.
Kurt was making God perceptible to the woman. Jesus walked into
the room through Kurt and expressed how he felt about the woman
and her traumatized life.

We asked the woman how she felt by Kurt's somewhat unusual ministry of tears. She was overwhelmed and greatly encouraged. It was the first time she felt that someone actually and deeply entered into her life struggle. Tears are the language of the soul.

The pastoral adventure is learning to perceive and report the Lord Jesus' walking-in-our-midst presence. It may be quiet and ordinary, or it may be unusual and full of tears (or laughter). Through the faithful practice of the disciplines, through the obedient use of spiritual gifts, through faith that activates all our capacity to perceive him, pastoring is bringing God to people. Our Chief Shepherd did just that. God visited us as the Word incarnate. As undershepherds our calling is the same.

I hope this extended conversation about Jesus as our Senior Pastor has encouraged you. I'm not asking that you agree with me in all that I have said, but that you would join with me in loving, worshiping, obeying, and becoming like our Chief Shepherd.

As I have emphasized, we are living in the transition to a new millennium. These are extraor-

> *Through the faithful practice of the disciplines, through the obedient use of spiritual gifts, through faith that activates all our capacity to perceive him, pastoring is bringing God to people.*

dinary days in which to live and serve Jesus Christ. I believe that the role of pastors and the mission of the church are going to recapture their place in our culture and world. Empowered pastors will lead the way as they follow Christ. To be sure, some of us may experience our own version of "exiled to Patmos" for the cause of Christ, but that will not stop the Chief Shepherd from showing up at specific locations on this planet.

What a grand calling it is to pastor! But one knotty issue must be faced: What gifts of the Spirit are operative in the contemporary church? This is subject of the next chapter.

JESUS AND HIS SPIRIT-EMPOWERED CHURCH

THE GIFTS OF THE SPIRIT

SHE sat across the desk from me in my office in Racine, Wisconsin. I was a recent graduate from Dallas Seminary, and she was somewhat new to the church. I was the youth pastor, and she was a young wife and mother who wanted to tell me a personal thing about her life. Sitting before me, looking over her shoulders both ways, she confided in me with a whisper that she spoke in tongues as a prayer language.

This was my first encounter with a real human being who "did it." Everything in my theology told me, "No, she did not 'do it,' because it is just not biblically done today."

I asked her to explain to me what she uttered in her "tongue." She took out a notebook and showed me the words. I saw syllables like "alleluia," "hallelu," and "hallel." What did I think? She wanted to know.

Ah, ha! Being an astute graduate of an Old Testament studies program, I discerned a strong Hebrew influence on her "tongue," her prayer language. She had written down syllables from the Hebrew language.

I said, "Is this it? This is your 'prayer language'?" She said that it was. I laughed to myself and felt a complete freedom to bless her and told her to practice her prayer language all she wanted. When she left I asked God to never let me rob any of his children of any gift they believe he has given.

Nothing quite like the question, "What New Testament gifts of the Spirit are still operative today?" can spark animated debates among evangelicals. Such a question, however, must be asked if we pastors are to engage the task facing us as we forge into the new millennium. In *Megatrends 2000*, Naisbitt and Aburdene note: "Religious belief is intensifying worldwide under the gravitational pull of the year 2000, the new millennium. When people are buffeted about by change, the need for spiritual belief intensifies."[1] With the intensification of this worldwide spiritual quest, the need for Spirit-empowered pastors skyrockets.

I was trained within a cessationist system of doctrine. A cessationist believes that some spiritual gifts evidencing a recognized expression of supernatural power were linked only to the apostles and died out with or even before the last apostle, John, died (ca. A.D. 90). These supernatural gifts ("sign gifts") were necessary, according to cessationist reasoning, until the canon of Scripture was completed and/or until Jerusalem, the base of Jewish unbelief, was destroyed under the Roman general Titus around A.D. 70.

I respect my training and those who capably trained me; however, I now reject cessationist views and the arguments for those views. I have become an evangelical noncessationist. I have reached this position, not only after extensive exegetical reconsideration, but from serious pastoral reflection as well. In the exegetical arena, competent pastor-scholars like D. A. Carson, Walter Bodine, Wayne Grudem, Jack Deere, Sam Storms, and Gordon Fee have pointed out the flimsy interpretive choices holding up the seemingly monolithic cessationist views. Scholars like these and others need to be honestly consulted for their biblical research and pastoral wisdom. Out of careful reexamination of crucial biblical texts regarding the spiritual gifts, an inexorable emergence of noncessationist evangelicalism is occurring.

> *Out of careful reexamination of crucial biblical texts regarding the spiritual gifts, an inexorable emergence of noncessationist evangelicalism is occurring.*

I recognize that exegetical choices have to be made, and while I respect those made by cessationist teachers and pastors, I have come to suspect those choices. I believe they reflect more of a cumbersome *pneumaphobia*, or "fear of the Spirit," than they reflect serious exegetical inquiry. D. A. Carson bluntly states that some cessationist reasoning reflects "exegetical naiveté."[2] Coming to noncessationist conclusions about the supernatural gifts has not transformed me, as may be popularly assumed, into either a Pentecostal or a "charismatic" as defined by John MacArthur in his book *Charismatic Chaos*.[3]

Since using "word pictures" is an effective way to get a crucial or difficult point across, I will use a word picture from the medical field to drive home what I believe is the very serious nature of excising even a few of the gifts of the Spirit. In using this word picture, I by no means intend disrespect to the Holy Spirit.

Men who do not want to reproduce children can undergo a minor outpatient surgical procedure called a vasectomy. Tubes in their reproductive organs are snipped and closed off making it almost totally impossible to procreate. They can function sexually, but their power to reproduce is gone.

Cessationism is a vasectomy of the Spirit. I am convinced that the cessationist position diminishes the potential of the Spirit's power in the church. It creates limits to the invading and life-changing power of the Spirit. This is not to say that cessationist believers and pastors live lives that are unchanged by the Spirit. I would never say that, because I do not believe that. The Spirit is recognized among them, worshiped as God, depended on for filling, and revered as the superintending source of inscripturated revelation, that is, the Scriptures. In fact, cessationists affirm all that the Bible affirms about the person and work of the Spirit except for the continuation of all the gifts of 1 Corinthians 12–14. This seems like a minor issue to cessationist proponents. A vasectomy is minor surgery, too, but the effects are considerable.

THREE DANGEROUS ATTITUDES

The cessationist system of "minor surgery" on the Spirit results in profoundly major and pastorally dangerous attitudes. Three attitudes that need to be admitted and dealt with are: (1) frustration, (2) suspicious fear, and, most seriously, (3) resisting the Holy Spirit.

Frustration results when people either read or hear about the manifest power and supernatural giftings in the early church and then are told that these encounters and giftings are not for believers today. People long (often secretly) for those same powerful realities in their own lives. Theological systems can blunt but cannot eradicate people's deep hunger for an extraordinary God working supernaturally in their lives. Yet trusted Bible teachers tell people that supernatural operations of the Spirit are not for today. People's minds dutifully accept the doctrines, but their hearts quietly yearn for the reality of the supernatural presence of God. And cessationist Christians, if alert, clearly hear and sometimes see that those alleged "temporary" gifts offer the reality of God's wonderful supernatural presence.

Honest people want to know why the supernatural gifts were for the apostles and the early church but supposedly are not for today. Cessationist teachers tell them something like this: "Because we have the completed canon of Scripture, we don't need dreams, prophetic revelations, healings, miracles, tongues, and interpretation of tongues. The early church did not have the completed Scriptures, so God allowed the supernatural gifts to function temporarily."

People today continue to wonder, however, about the state of their own lives and the low moral character of the church. Today's church, like the early church, has to contend with Satan's blinding, human depravity's deceitfulness, and the relentless crush of a fallen world system. Evangelical believers can plainly see that the church is collapsing on every side, all the while holding the completed canon (the Bible) in their hands. It is obvious to all but the cessationists, apparently, that not only do we need all of the Bible, we also need all of the gifts of the one who inspired it. We need the powerful supernatural manifestations of the Holy Spirit, who speaks directly and works miraculously *today*.

Sadly, people are told that they cannot have such a Spirit. They are told that the Holy Spirit works differently by not working *as fully* as he did in the first century. Some very good people, believing these things, still cannot escape their longing for the Spirit and for supernatural reality. They yearn for the Spirit who communicates God's personal and immediate presence by working through supernatural gifts.

Gerald Hawthorne calls the contemporary church into the full experience of the Holy Spirit's empowerment.

> *There is no reason whatsoever to believe that what was true of those earliest Christians is any less true of Christians in this century. Surely contemporary crises are no less great, the pains of the world no less meliorated, the challenges to one's strength, wisdom, patience, and love no less demanding of resources beyond human resources than they were in the first century, and followers of Jesus today are no more sufficient for all these in and of themselves than his followers yesterday. Furthermore, God's program of enabling people to burst the bounds of their human limitations and achieve the impossible is still in place and still effective—that program that involves filling people with his Spirit, filling them with supernatural powers.*[4]

Dallas Willard, in his discussion of the ways that God does still speak today apart from the canon of Scripture, warns: "From the pastoral point of view, one of the greatest harms we can do to those under our care is to convince them that God is not going to meet them personally in their experience, or that He is *really* doing so only if we approve of what is happening."[5]

Of course, those who teach cessationism would say that this frustration, born out of unfulfilled longing created by the minor theological surgery on the Holy Spirit, never was their intent. Nevertheless, they must live with the creation of a deep-felt frustration, bordering on resentment in some people. We cannot curb the Spirit's ministry even a little bit ("Just some gifts are inoperable today") in the name of good systematic theology without facing pastorally disastrous consequences.

> We cannot curb the Spirit's ministry even a little bit . . . in the name of good systematic theology without facing pastorally disastrous consequences.

FEAR THAT DIVIDES

A second pastorally dangerous attitude resulting from cessationist views is *suspicious fear*. The theological diversity in the evangelical world is becoming well recognized by the men and women in our churches. Not only diversity of doctrine, but diversity of experience is becoming widely and curiously noted. The phenomenon of Promise Keepers has facilitated biblical unity among Christian men who represent wide spectrums of theological and denominational diversity. Many people in cessationist churches are becoming good friends with noncessationist brothers and sisters. Comparing one another's encounters with the Spirit is inevitable. Cessationist believers can only assign suspicion-breeding, fearful reasons to their noncessationist friends' experiences with the Spirit. They say such things as, "It's shallow emotionalism, or worse, it's demonic."

Cessationist believers are discovering, however, that their Christian noncessationist friends are not wild-eyed lunatics. They are not driven to seek emotional and spiritual highs. And they certainly are not demonized. They are simply Spirit-filled believers who love God and love people.

Cessationism, by its nature, however, insinuates something like, "Yeah, but they believe in prophecy and healing and words of knowledge and real 'demonic warfare.' There must be something wrong with them. Why do they violate the assured truth that the Spirit does *not* give and work through supernatural gifts today?" Questions like these are symptomatic of a divisive, suspicion-breeding fear.

Could this suspicious fear be included in what Charles Swindoll, now president of Dallas Seminary, is referring to in a *Christianity Today* interview in which he was asked, "Will Dallas Seminary ever make friends with charismatics?" Swindoll said, "If you read my newest book, *Flying Closer to the Flame*, you'd probably think it sounds like a softening of my position on the Holy Spirit. I think the school [Dallas Theological Seminary] without knowing it probably operated from a standpoint of fear—fear of being misunderstood, of things getting out of control, of losing doctrinal distinctives. I don't think we need to be afraid. There's wider room for interpretation than we may have allowed"[6]

This is a truly perceptive pastoral response about a highly esteemed Christian enterprise, Dallas Seminary. Swindoll's statements help break open the discussion about the Holy Spirit and allow for ongoing, loving dialogue. As pastoral comments they carry tremendous wisdom. Just imagine: If a seminary operates out of fear, what do you suppose grips the people in the churches?

Another pastor, Charles Stanley, writing about the absence of fear in relationship to the Holy Spirit, observes:

> *Surrendered men and women who have given over control of their lives to the Savior welcome the Father's will.* They are not afraid of the Spirit's leading. *They are not threatened. Why? Because Jesus is not threatened by the will of the Father. And when Jesus sits as Lord on the throne of a life, He is never threatened by the will of the Father from that vantage point, either (emphasis mine).*[7]

Again, cessationist proponents would deny that creating suspicious fear is their intent. But pastors who are out in the trenches hear the stories of what cessationism does in yearning hearts. Pastors discover that thinking people get extremely tired of trying to sort through all the intricate theological maneuvers used to buttress cessationism and become wearied by the continued (sometimes hostile) division over what certainly should be a uniting reality—the "unity *of the Spirit* through the bond of peace" (Eph. 4:3, italics mine). Wearied people today are very similar to those in Jesus' day, "harassed and helpless" (Matt. 9:36), needing an empowered shepherd to lead them.

Harassed by evangelical infighting over gifts and helpless in the face of a weakened church (with their own vacant lives as evidence), a third negative consequence of cessationist theology erupts in people. It is perhaps the most dangerous result of all: *resisting the Holy Spirit.*

We need all the gifts of the Spirit to reach *the goal* of the gifts. The goal of the gifts is Christlikeness, which grows not only as the Spirit evidences his "fruit" in human lives, but also as he expresses his power, sometimes in supernatural ways. In rejecting such supernatural expressions, cessationists are in danger of not only resisting the gifts the Spirit gives, but stunting at best and outright rejecting at worst the resulting Christlikeness the gifts are designed to produce (see Rom. 8:29; Eph. 4:13). The Father's sovereign, predestined purpose for his children is handicapped by the removal of even a few of the gifts. Cessationism becomes serious tampering with the biblically based, Spirit-given means for fulfilling God's transforming purpose in salvation.

When it comes to the gifts of the Spirit, rather than fostering attitudes like frustration, suspicious fear, and resisting the Spirit, does not the New Testament invite us to cultivate attitudes of fulfillment and contentment, acceptance of one another, and surrendering completely to the control of the Spirit with a joyful expectancy to see him work? I am not asking for "peace at any price" in the body of Christ; I am asking us (especially pastors) to "make every effort to keep the unity of the Spirit through the bond of peace" (Eph. 4:3).

> *The Spirit of God, in sovereign freedom, "colors outside the lines" of our so-called systematic categories.*

Many other former cessationists and I have come to realize that the Spirit is giving all the gifts regardless of the tenets of anyone's systematic theology. The Spirit of God, in sovereign freedom, "colors outside the lines" of our so-called systematic categories. The Spirit is operating in today's church just as Old Testament prophets predicted he would operate under the new covenant (see Joel 2; Acts 2), just as Jesus said he would (John 14–17), and as Acts and the New Testament letters testify he would. What an untamed Spirit he is to not act "decently and in order" with regard to our fine theological distinctives.

READY FOR THE FINALE

The church is hurtling toward history's grand finale, the *parousia* of Jesus Christ and the establishment of the millennium. The Spirit is working under Jesus Christ's direction to prepare Christ's bride, the church, to be presented to his Father. As this purpose reaches its climax, Satan will frantically do all that he can to frustrate that purpose.

In his wild frustration, Satan will become more extroverted in his attempts. He will become more daring and public in his demonic plan to keep people blinded to Christ. It is for such a time as this that the

Spirit enables the church to arise, face the Enemy and, with supernatural empowerment, engage the forces of darkness. Indeed, as Martin Luther penned ages ago concerning the Christian mission in a devil-filled world, "The Spirit *and the gifts* are ours, through him who with us sideth" (italics mine)!

The Spirit of God is empowering the church with supernatural gifts whether our theology allows for it or not. The Spirit distributes the gifts as he determines (1 Cor. 12:11). This fact calls the people of God to face "the line in the sand" drawn by the Spirit himself. Will we stay on our side of the line, resisting his call to greater empowerment? Will we forfeit this empowerment because of the limitations imposed on us by our systematic theologies? Will we continue to be so brazen as to say, "The Spirit can't be operating this way today, *our* theological categories won't allow for it"? Or will we cross the line into the reality of what the Spirit is doing all around us and allow a wideness in our systematic theology that accounts for the reality? Not all believers have to experience all the gifts, but all the gifts must be allowed for, biblically defined and faithfully deployed, within the church.

Cessationists, probably with sincere humility, say, "We would never conclude that God *can't* give whatever gifts he chooses to give. We just believe, for what to us are good theological reasons, that he has chosen to withdraw some of them." In light of the escalating emergence of noncessationist evangelicalism, a wiser cessationist restatement might be something like, "Because we believe that the sovereign God can give whatever gifts he chooses to give, it certainly appears that he once again is giving all the gifts to the church." The "once again" lets the cessationists save face in light of the undeniable reality of the Spirit's bestowal of all the gifts of 1 Corinthians 12:7–11 on the contemporary church. (Of course, our traditional Pentecostal and charismatic brothers and sisters don't need a "once again" in their discussion of gifts.)

Nothing seems more spiritually dangerous than haranguing members of the body of Christ for what the Spirit himself is doing. We must never overlook that gifts are described as a "manifestation of the Spirit" (1 Cor. 12:7). Yet a divisive and tolerated haranguing goes on by well-known, popular Christian leaders. I now believe all such verbal and written assaults may not be the evidence of well-meaning attempts at "defending the faith," but may actually be a resisting of the Spirit. May God have mercy on us all.

Our (sometimes angry) disagreements over the Spirit and the gifts he gives are a different kind of argument than other differences we voice. We tolerate considerable differences over modes of baptism, the practice of the Lord's Table, forms of ecclesiastical government, and various translations of the Bible (for example, the KJV versus the NIV), just to name a few. Spiritual gifts, however, are not about a ritual or a debated viewpoint of polity or a systematic doctrine. *The gifts are about a person, the Third Person of the Holy Trinity.* Gifts are about how the Spirit operates. We must never allow our systematic theology to serve as (even minor) surgery on the Spirit of God. We dare not presume to be doctors excising from the Spirit and his ministry anything that we do not have clear, indisputable grounds for excising.

> *We must never allow our systematic theology to serve as (even minor) surgery on the Spirit of God.*

Cessationist arguments are not always clear and certainly are not indisputable. I have come to realize that my former cessationist views put me at once on both very thin ice and holy ground regarding spiritual gifts. It is not enough to say, "Although the sign gifts died in the first century, the Holy Spirit did not."[8] Spiritual gifts, and in particular the so-called sign gifts, are clearly defined by Paul as manifestations of the resident Holy Spirit. They are evidences of his personal presence operating to expand the lordship of Christ in the church. It's simple: To the degree you do away with spiritual gifts, to the same degree you do away with the Spirit. And remember, one of his titles is "the Spirit of Jesus" (Acts 16:7).

I write as one pastor reflecting on what I believe is a serious weakness in American evangelical theology. Cessationism is a handicapped system. Cessationism not only produces a cauldron of negative attitudes that cause the people in our churches to forfeit dimensions of empowerment and development of authentic Christlikeness; it spawns a real loss for pastors too. This loss extends as well to their pastoral ministry. This loss, largely not spoken about because of evangelical peer pressure, must be honestly faced.

The peer pressure among pastors today is reminiscent of the pressure put on people in Jesus' day. The first-century religious leaders spat out their theologically controlling question to the guards who did not arrest Jesus: "Has any of the rulers or the Pharisees believed in him?" (John 7:48). In other words, they were saying, "Get with the program. We've got the truth. Dare you insult us with a change in your thinking? Just believe what we tell you."

Cessationism leaves pastors with the Spirit, yes, but a Spirit clipped down and relegated to one specific ministry: to transform pastor and people into an unfinished image of Jesus. The Spirit's primary role becomes that of making us like Jesus only in character. And that character development is void of any demonstrable displays of supernatural power.

I am certainly not saying that Christlike character development is wrong, for obviously it is not. It is, however, shortsighted. It leaves Christians with an inward focus solely on the Spirit's work—a focus that easily mutates into self-absorption. Such a limited view centers only on the "fruit of the Spirit" (Gal. 5:22–23), and shaping the character of Jesus in us becomes the essential and only functional operation of the Spirit. This is incomplete and ineffective, for Christlike character is only half of what Christlikeness involves.

Even with the primary focus on "the fruit of the Spirit" in cessationist theology, Christian people are starkly aware today of the serious absence of true and enduring holiness in their lives. The promise of the Christlikeness they long for and are told is theirs is not experienced.

Most pastors cannot escape the latest polling data, those statistical voices of doom detailing how the evangelical church is like the world in almost every measurable category. Sadly, we are in the world and *of* it. Many pastors, wearied from hearing incessant reports about the church's "dark side," dejectedly turn away from their high pastoral calling and quit.

Aware of and admitting the anemic condition of the evangelical church, some leaders cry out, "What we need is more passionate expository preaching of the Word!" Surely, they contend, sound preaching will solve the moral crises in the church. But any alert observer of the evangelical church will report that biblical truth is preached passionately from evangelical pulpits. To its credit, the evangelical church is stellar in its commitment to guarding and transmitting the content of biblical truth.

Nevertheless, the transmitting of truth is not leading to the transforming of lives. Many pastors, after years of splendid expository preaching, sit at their desks and wonder, *Where are the changed lives?* Even more pointedly, they do personal inventory and weep in the night, "Where, O God, is the reality of my own changed life?"

Genuinely Spirit-gifted pastors and churches cannot be satisfied with aiming to be like Jesus in character alone. Pastors and people are designed and called to be like Jesus in power as well. Isn't it obvious by now that we cannot truly have his character without his power? Sadly, cessationist theology steals that hope away. Empowered pastors have a God-given inner desire not only to be like Christ in character, but also to minister like Christ in power through the gifts of the Spirit.

> *Empowered pastors have a God-given inner desire not only to be like Christ in character, but also to minister like Christ in power through the gifts of the Spirit.*

LIKE CHRIST IN POWER

The uniquely supernatural gifts of the Spirit given to the church offer pastors and people fulfillment for the deep desire to be like Christ in power. They serve to bring the immediacy and intimacy of God's loving and powerful presence. These gifts have nothing to do with television personalities who are self-promoting, prosperity-preaching, manipulative "healers." These gifts are for quiet, gentle, and relatively obscure pastors and people living out their lives in that realm erupting with divine life that Jesus and Paul proclaimed as "the kingdom of God."

If the more supernatural gifts (those listed in 1 Cor. 12–14) died with the apostles (or before), with what do we replace the loss of a supernatural ministry? We replace it with more training (note the meteoric rise in doctor of ministry degree programs), more seminars, more books, more sharpening of our communication skills, more market analyses, more techniques and trends to consider, and more angry arguments and tabloid-style denunciations spewed out about those jumping ship from cessationism.

Often those Christian traditions, like Pentecostalism for example, that exhibit a passionate hunger and thirst for God are held suspect for their imprecise theology of *more*.[9] As an evangelical noncessationist, I have come to the conclusion that "more" of the Spirit is exactly what we need. What a great replacement for all the "mores" of cessationism! After all, improving pastoral techniques is simply improving pastoral techniques. Gaining more knowledge is just gaining more knowledge. These things bring no improvement to the soul. "Obviously a wise heart does not refer to knowledge, skill, technique, or the capacity to control. Instead, it seems to mean a capacity to submit, relinquish, and acknowledge the decisive impingement of Yahweh on one's life."[10]

Jesus, to be the Christ, the Anointed One, needed the Spirit of God. The Spirit came upon and anointed Jesus to fulfill his mission as the Christ. In his humanity and as our example, he needed and depended on the Spirit for ministry, undeniably a supernatural ministry. How can we, his undershepherds, need the Spirit any less?

My prayer is that as you read this, you will sense a hopeful question forming in your heart: "Could there be *more* for me and my ministry than what I am so frustratingly used to?" Regrettably, I suspect that some readers are shaking their wizened pastoral heads and thinking: *Oh no, here's another one awash in a theology of experience and abandoning the "assured results" of the best exegetical reformed and dispensational minds. Just watch where he ends up. Time will surely tell.*

But as Bob Dylan sings, "The times, they are a-changin'." I was taken by surprise a few years ago when I read a quote in *Christianity Today* by Dr. Charles Ryrie, a former Dallas Theological Seminary professor of mine and stellar evangelical voice for dispensationalism. Ryrie said: "I do not think dispensationalism as a system of theology *requires the cessation of gifts*. Some dispensationalists believe some gifts have ceased, and that they can support this exegetically and historically. But I don't think the system requires that" (italics mine).[11] I doubt that Dr. Ryrie agrees with where I, as a Dallas graduate, have landed regarding the sign gifts, but I thank him for his honesty about the doctrinal system he advocates and defends. Pastors today can actually be noncessationist dispensationalists. What a great era in which to live and minister!

Spirit-empowerment exhibited in all the gifts of the Spirit described in 1 Corinthians 12–14 invites the church not only into Christlike character, but also into Christlike ministry. These gifts, supposedly relegated to the first century, were given *to the church*,[12] not just to the apostles. These gifts are being rediscovered and used by noncessationist exegetical scholars and pastors and by laypeople but without the unbiblical assertions and unwise excesses characteristic of some noncessationist traditions. These gifts, like any of the gifts, become dangerous only when severed from Christ's loving lordship and from caring (and careful) pastoral ministry. Pentecostal scholar Gordon Fee wisely writes:

> *The presence of the Spirit in power and gifts makes it easy for God's people to think of the power and the gifts as the real evidence of the Spirit's presence. Not so for Paul. The ultimate criterion of the Spirit's activity is the exaltation of Jesus as Lord. Whatever takes away from that, even if they be legitimate expressions of the Spirit, begins to move away from Christ to a more pagan fascination with spiritual activity as an end in itself.*[13]

The Chief Shepherd intends for his undershepherds to serve under him with the same supernatural empowerment for ministry as he had. Pastors, along with growing in Christlike character, are to be serving with Christlike power. We are to be empowered pastors.

WHAT IS EMPOWERMENT?

What do I mean by empowered? I do not mean that pastors who hold cessationist views of the sign gifts are without the Spirit personally or in ministry. I believe they are bringing glory to the Father and are obedient to Jesus Christ. I am convinced, however, that they forfeit wonderful dimensions of pastoral empowerment because of their cessationist persuasion. Losses occur in the spiritual realm when the Spirit's ministry to and through the church is partially removed with the scalpel of cessationist theological thinking.

Nor do I mean by empowered that all pastors themselves must or do possess the more supernatural gifts. Yet some pastors may possess some of them, and all certainly are encouraged by Paul to seek them (1 Cor. 12:31; 14:1).

What I do mean by empowered is that all pastors are invited to minister among and oversee churches in which all the gifts are being given today. With a seeking heart and openness to the Spirit, any pastor can be part of a community of believers that is fully empowered for significant Christlike ministry.

My primary spiritual gift is teaching. I will not knowingly tolerate something promoted as a "biblical truth" unless I am convinced it has a sound exegetical base. I have been trained well in the "normal hermeneutic" of conservative evangelicalism. I have tended to lean more toward biblical theology, that is, toward grasping the theology of the biblical authors, than toward systematic theology. Of course I do see the value in systematics and have been helped by Wayne Grudem's contribution[14] to evangelical systematics as he presents arguments for noncessationist interpretations.

The danger I see in systematics is that the system may at times supersede the biblical text and may become a lens through which the Scriptures are read. This becomes high-powered but nonetheless blatant *eisegesis*. (*Eisegesis* is "reading into" the text a meaning that is not there, as opposed to *exegesis*, which is "reading out" of the biblical text what the original authors intended.) Eisegesis can create interpretations of the text based on the system rather than letting the biblical text shape and modify the system.

Having been trained in some pretty elaborate exegetical maneuvers to conclude that some gifts are not given today, I now shake my head at them. All the primary texts (and there aren't that many) allegedly teaching that some gifts have ceased may be read in very simple and straightforward ways resulting in sound exegetical reasons why all the spiritual gifts are operative today. For example, Paul's statement that "tongues, then, are a sign . . . for unbelievers " (1 Cor. 14:22) goes on an amazing roller-coaster ride in the cessationist system. It is first linked to Jewish unbelief because of the preceding quote of Isaiah 28:11–12, that unbelief is tied to the Jewish rejection of Jesus. This Jewish rejection of Jesus is then welded to Jesus' prediction of Jerusalem's destruction, which occurred in A.D. 70; and since Jerusalem, the center of Jewish unbelief is destroyed in A.D. 70, then tongues, which serve as a sign for *Jewish* unbelievers (which Paul never said), are no longer needed. Therefore, the gift of tongues is rendered obsolete. Whoa, is the ride over yet? This whole "house of cards" of cessationist argumentation is soundly answered by New Testament exegetical scholars like D. A. Carson and Gordon Fee.[15]

An alert cessationist reader may ask at this point, "What about the gift of 'apostle'?" The term *apostle* has several levels of meaning, and, no, I do not believe *apostle* in the technical sense of one of the Twelve is applicable today. Careful New Testament study shows that the semantic range of the term extends beyond the Twelve. Jack Deere has an insightful discussion of the term *apostle* in his book *Surprised by the Power of the Spirit.*[16]

By empowered pastors, I mean undershepherds who are gifted or who oversee people who are gifted by the Spirit to bring real, demonstrable expressions of supernatural power into the life and ministry of the church. "Skillful shepherds will be sensitive to the wind of the Spirit. This will lead to a new flexibility of operation and to an all-round ministry where there is no divorce between the spoken word of God and the miraculous work of the Spirit."[17]

> By empowered pastors, I mean undershepherds who are gifted ... to bring real, demonstrable expressions of supernatural power into the life and ministry of the church.

EQUIPPED TO DO WHAT JESUS DID

The diagram below demonstrates that common ministries are shared by Spirit-empowered servants. God has equipped the church through the Spirit to do the things that Jesus did. It is very clear that at least three Spirit-empowered ministries are held in common: proclaiming the kingdom of God, healing diseases, and exorcising demons. The purpose of the diagram is to show that the church *as a community* is empowered by the Spirit of God with spiritual gifts that equip the church to do the "works" as well as to proclaim the "words" of Jesus. Broadly, then, the church is empowered to "be like Jesus" with regard to both proclamation ministries and demonstrations of power ministries.

	JESUS	THE 12	THE 72	CHURCH IN ACTS	CHURCH IN CORINTH
Proclaiming the kingdom of God: Forgiveness	Luke 6:20; 9:11, 27; 11:20	Luke 9:2,6	Luke 10:9	Acts 8:12; 19:8; 28:31	1 Cor. 4:20; 6:9–10; 15:24, 50
Healing	Luke 4:40; 5:15; 6:19	Luke 9:2,6	Luke 10:9	Acts 3:6–10; 4:30; 5:16; 19:11–12	1 Cor. 12:9 "Gifts of healings" (James 5:15–17)
Exorcising "Spiritual warfare"	Luke 4:33–37, 41; 6:18; 8:26–39	Luke 9:1	Luke 10:17	Acts 5:16; 19:12–16	1 Cor. 12:10 "Miraculous powers," "distinguishing between spirits."

The common ministries of Spirit-empowered servants who live like Jesus

One expression of empowerment to proclaim the presence of God and his kingdom is prophetic revelations of various kinds. While the New Testament does not exhaustively define the gifts "word/message of wisdom" and "word/message of knowledge," (1 Cor. 12:8), many believe that these two gifts are subsets or subcategories of prophetic revelation. Gifts of healing are still given today, as well as the gifts of discerning spirits in the realm of spiritual warfare, faith (the kind that trusts God for the impossible, 1 Cor. 13:1–3), working miracles, speaking in "spiritual languages" (to use Pastor Jack Hayford's phrase for "tongues"), and interpreting those languages for the benefit of the corporate body of believers (see 1 Cor. 12:7–11).

Jesus modeled empowered ministry and invites his undershepherds into the same kind of ministry by gifting his church with authentic Spirit empowerment. Seeing the silhouette of a jet in my mind's eye while in prayer for Cathy was a "revelation" from the Spirit that enabled me to shepherd her into forgiveness and peace with God.

Texts in the Gospels that have often been interpreted as expressions of Jesus' omniscience (and, therefore, arguments for his deity) are sometimes nothing more than prophetic revelation given to Jesus by the Spirit. As a case in point, consider again the story of the woman at the well in John 4. When Jesus revealed to her that he had knowledge of her five previous husbands and that she presently was living with a man who was not her husband, what did the woman say? She didn't gasp, drop to her knees, and say, "Oh, no! I'm in the presence of an omniscient God!" She said, "Sir, I perceive that you are *a prophet.*" Her biblical category of "prophet" allowed for Jesus' reception and reporting of detailed revealed information, information she thought was forever concealed in her soul. This Samaritan woman had good biblical theology about "prophet," though in other ways her theology was deficient, for example, regarding worship, as Jesus himself pointed out.

No evangelical pastor should proceed into ministry today without wrestling with the emergence of new understandings of the gifts of the Spirit listed in 1 Corinthians 12–14. Prophecy in the New Testament is greatly distorted by cessationist arguments. New Testament prophesying does not compete with nor threaten inscripturated revelation as cessationists so strongly suggest. Wayne Grudem's extensive study of biblical prophecy leads him to provide a provocative definition for the New Testament gift of prophecy. "On the other side, I am asking those in the cessationist camp to give serious thought to the possibility that prophecy in ordinary New Testament churches was not equal to Scripture in authority, but was simply a very human—and sometimes partially mistaken—report of something the Holy Spirit brought to someone's mind."[18]

If the New Testament gift of prophecy given to believers is defined as reporting in human words what the Holy Spirit spontaneously brings to mind (as Grudem argues), how is this really any different from what Dr. Charles Swindoll describes as Holy Spirit-given "revelations" in the counseling process? Swindoll, in an interview with *Christian Counseling Today*, testified:

> *I remain very sensitive to these inner promptings. . . . I think that during those times, the Spirit of God brings to my attention either biblical principles, scriptural statements, or some comment that I would not otherwise have had. . . . [W]e should not hold back but should say the things that come to mind. . . . He [the Spirit] reveals the things we should know. So when they are revealed, he deserves the credit for those revelations or understanding.*[19]

Swindoll, I believe, is using the terms *revealed* and *revelations*, not in the sense of providing truth equivalent in authority to the inscripturated Word (the Bible), but in the less technical sense of reporting in human words "what the Spirit brings to mind." Reporting these promptings, impulses, scriptural statements, principles, comments, revelations, and understanding is the essence of the New Testament gift of prophecy.

My inner vision of a jet while in prayer was something the Spirit brought spontaneously to mind (or "revealed"), and I reported it. It was truly revelational in nature. God gave it, and Cathy was encouraged and comforted. "But everyone who prophesies speaks to men for their strengthening, encouragement and comfort" (1 Cor. 14:3).

Jesus healed diseases, discerned spirits (and exorcised them), spoke prophetic revelations, and did miraculous deeds. He invites the church into such a ministry and equips the church to do it. Empowered pastors will affirm these dimensions of ministry while trying to maintain a balance in their expression.

Some evangelical believers argue for tongues as the sign of the baptism of the Holy Spirit. While some say, "That's extreme!" we must recognize our differences in the larger context of the theological traditions within the body of Christ and say more irenically, "That's different, and I will agree to disagree." Finding a demon behind every bush, behind every aspect of Christian deficiency is extreme, but learning about and engaging in spiritual warfare is a vital part of Christian growth. Claiming that God *must* heal all diseases now is extreme, but praying for healings with faith-filled expectancy is our joyful freedom. The extremes can be biblically and pastorally answered without having to resort to the cumbersome and elaborate cessationist structure to do away with the sign gifts.

> As our world's pursuit of spiritual reality reaches a fever pitch, pastors will need greater empowerment by the Spirit for their task.

As the new millennium unfolds and as our world's pursuit of spiritual reality reaches a fever pitch, pastors will need greater empowerment by the Spirit for their task. Fortunately, the power of the Holy Spirit is abundantly available. The Holy

Spirit empowers the church with all the gifts in order to equip the church to get the job done. The church is called to bring Jesus Christ's deeply liberating salvation to those needing and seeking God. Along with the proclamation of sound doctrine, the church will be called to minister with demonstrations of supernatural power in a world where the "saved and unsaved, [are] starving for an extraordinary glimpse of God."[20]

JESUS AND COMMUNITY

How Jesus Shepherds
His Undershepherds

I was desperate. I would wander down into our basement and mull over how I could cleanly commit suicide. I have a little .410 shotgun, but I concluded that it would be too messy and too loud. Plus, I was too much of a chicken to kill myself that way. I conjured up too many scenarios that were repulsive. A neighbor down the street had killed himself by sitting in his car in the garage with the engine running. That seemed clean and easy. What should I do? All I knew for sure was that I needed "to get out." What about Julie? What about my four lovely daughters (if one of them found me dead)? What about the church? What was I thinking to contemplate such a selfish and hateful act? Down, down, I spiraled in dark dread and guilt.

The desperation that flowed through my veins, pulsating with every beat of my heart, stemmed from an ugly mixture of failed expectations, out-of-control feelings of inadequacy, sheer boredom with pastoring (no longer my calling, just "my job"), and the accusations of the Enemy, who spewed out encouragements to do myself in because I was no good ("The thief comes only to . . . kill," John 10:10).

I was meeting weekly for breakfast with a fellow elder in our church to discuss leadership issues. To summarize our seemingly unending discussions, my fellow elder concluded that although I was a good teacher and a somewhat fair pastor, I wasn't a good leader. In fact, I swung and missed every pitch as a leader. Needless to say, getting up early in the morning for that breakfast meeting wasn't the highlight of my week.

People were leaving the church. They didn't like the way things were done in the children's ministry, the youth ministry, and the music ministry. They didn't like our church's view on baptism, on the Lord's Table, on elder rule. You name it—it wasn't being done right. Out of my own brokenness, I concluded that all these things were my fault. I wasn't a good leader.

These were the months when I hated preaching. Because God's truth wasn't working in and for me, I hated to get up and tell people of his love and his ability to change lives. I felt I was a piece of church equipment, functioning in my role as "the good Bible teacher."

I believed I was failing Julie, my girls, and the church. I believed I was failing the elders and the church staff. And most horrible thought of all, I believed I was failing God. Every direction I turned, I saw only failure. I was desperate. What I didn't know was that all these beliefs were lies.

I finally mustered enough courage to write a brief note telling the good-intentioned elder that I couldn't meet with him for breakfast anymore. The meetings were doing us no good. It was evident to me that I was disappointing him and he was misunderstanding me. My decision to stop meeting offended him deeply, and he left the church. The Destroyer whispered in my ear, "I told you so. You are not a leader, just like he said. You even drove him from the church. Go ahead, make my day. Get out!"

This is difficult to describe now, but I remember the dreadful and relentless assault of depressing feelings of failure. Pressure would build in me to the point I felt extreme panic inside. I was failing as the "nice guy," the peacemaking pastor-teacher. Suicide seemed so reasonable.

One evening I was lying on the bed while Julie was downstairs watching television. I was feeling crushed inside, wasted. Julie didn't know any of this. As I lay there, a hymn from my youth came into my mind totally unbeckoned. It began strolling through the darkness of my soul, casting rays of light and hope. "Are we weak and heavy laden, cumbered with a load of care? Precious Savior, still our refuge; take it to the Lord in prayer." I began to sob. Precious Jesus. Jesus. Pain that I could no longer avoid came to the surface. I had to tell someone—someone who would listen to me like Jesus did.

I went downstairs to Julie. Crying as I talked, I told her I had to speak to her about something. Julie sensed something serious was happening as she saw and heard me in such a mess.

"What's wrong, John? What has happened? Have you been with another woman?"

"No, Julie, it's not that. I haven't been with a woman. I am so horribly depressed. I am such a failure. I am failing everyone in my life."

I rehearsed for her the litany of my feelings of failure. I spoke out the things that were shredding me to pieces inside—things about my inferiority, the people leaving the church, the thoughts of suicide. I had to get these things out of the darkness and into the light.

Julie, Julie. Bless her heart. She sat and listened, alarmed at times, but accepting. When I finished, she took me back through each issue of my desperation one at a time. She asked one simple question, "Now, John, how is this *your fault?* "

With a wisdom that is just short of miraculous, Julie's questions helped me separate the ministry and life issues with which I struggled. Like a skilled mechanic, using questions like tools, she took apart my tangled soul. I had become completely out of touch with who I was and completely overwhelmed by what I had (or had not) done. I had built an identity on performance, and when the grades were very low, as I felt they were, I concluded that I was a failure. I had assumed the blame for things that were totally beyond my control and responsibility.

That conversation with Julie helped me turn a corner. I had more soul repair, of course, but at least the cat was out of the bag regarding my desperate state.

Precious Jesus, still my refuge, visited and shepherded me. How? First, while lying on a bed of sorrow, an old hope-bringing, Jesus-affirming hymn, aroused and dancing once again in my spirit, brought God's light into my darkness. Second, Jesus in Julie listened, reasoned, and probed, bringing a sense of sanity to my very convoluted thinking. I, a pastor, was pastored.

SUPPORTED, CONNECTED

So, who pastors the pastor? This is a crucial question, for it bears on the health and survival of the pastor and on the well-being of the church under his or her charge. A line from a song I learned at Promise Keepers says, "No man is an island; no man stands alone." This line makes the point well, and it certainly applies to women pastors too. "The wolf gets the lone sheep."

Since those desperate days when suicide seemed so appealing, I have been deeply grateful for several levels of support that are in place for me. Without these supportive, enriching relationships, I believe I could detour once again down the dark road of dread. I could be driven to bail out or burn out of pastoral ministry.

Larry Crabb is so convinced that we need supportive, redemptive relationships that he has written a book about them called *Connecting: A Radical New Vision*. He writes: "I suggest that the absolute center of all powerful attempts to impact people for good is connecting. . . . Disconnected people are unaware of what God has placed within them that if poured into others could change lives. They feel either inadequate for questionable reasons or powerful for wrong reasons."[1]

First, and most importantly, every pastor must be pastored by Jesus himself. He is, after all, the Pastor of Pastors. As we considered the spiritual disciplines, we were impressed with Jesus' consistent and intimate union with the Father. Likewise, all pastors who long to be like Christ must cultivate a genuine, intimate conversational relationship with God. Reading Scripture and great devotional classics, praying psalms back to God, worshiping the Father, journaling our spiritual experiences—all these and many other practices can be very effective in helping us to have encounters with God that leave us refreshed, recharged, and ready to face the challenges of our calling.

> First, and most importantly, every pastor must be pastored by Jesus himself. He is, after all, the Pastor of Pastors.

Jesus has a passionate love for his undershepherds, and he longs to express his great Shepherd's heart to each one who takes up the calling to "feed the flock." Recall that it was honest love—"Peter, do you love me?"—that qualified Peter for his shepherding responsibilities.

As we develop a love relationship with Jesus, he will pastor us and send us out into a "field of souls" in partnership with him.

Pastors and their spouses need to be pastored in a small group. We all require a setting in which we can express our needs, be transparent, and receive the love and pastoring of Jesus through *"his body"*— other brothers and sisters in Christ. Julie and I are very thankful to be part of a loving small group in which we exuberantly worship, pray for and receive prayer from others, practice the gifts of the Spirit, and, frankly, can just "be." This kind of "house church" experience is vital for pastoral survival.

Our house church meeting usually includes singing some praise and worship songs accompanied by CD. We can sing as loud and as long as we want. We can bow down, kneel, clap, and dance. We can shout, cry, be silent, and, as our worship pastor colorfully says, "worship our guts out." It's great!

Then we may spend time in prayer, adoring God, blessing his name, and recounting his great qualities and deeds. We may move into a time of listening prayer in which someone receives a "word," sees a "picture," or senses an impression from God.[2] In the security and trust of the house church, we are free to explore what it means for Jesus to literally be among us and communicate his heart to us.

One evening a "picture" came to one of the older and wiser members of our group. He said, "Does anyone see the key, like the key to a members windup toy on Mike's back? I believe God is telling Mike [not his real name] that he has all kinds of stress in his life. He's feeling like a machine just going through the motions. God wants to bring to Mike supernatural peace."

Mike was floored. This was his first time to meet this older Christian. Mike operates a heart-lung machine while surgeons do open-heart surgery (an occupation permeated with stress). Mike was also tangled in a messy process of trying to sell his home and simplify his family's life (even more stress). He felt exactly like a toy wound tight, moving mechanically through life. The picture couldn't have been more accurate.

We put Mike on the "prayer bench," gathered around him, and began intercessory prayer. That night Mike knew that God loved him with a special, specific love, and Mike knew that God was on his side, for him, not against him.

You can't help but be renewed, refreshed, "pastored" in settings like that. Every pastor needs to be involved in a small, worshiping, caring, praying group.

I also thank God for a small group of men with whom I meet. (I'm sure that women pastors also benefit from being nurtured in a small group of their own gender.) My spiritual growth received a tremendous boost when I became an active participant in a men's small group. There is something about "ritual space," a time and place where men can be open and honest with other men. In my men's group, I am not there primarily as "the pastor" or "the teacher." I am just one of the guys, who needs to open up and be real with other men. In view of many of my personal struggles related to father issues, participating in a men's group has been vital for my emotional and spiritual health.

> *Every pastor needs to be involved in a small, worshiping, caring, praying group.*

NO LONE RANGERS

Another significant supportive relationship in my life and ministry is our church staff, which serves as a ministry team. While we all have individual spiritual gifts to use in ministry and different responsibilities to fulfill, none of us are "Lone Rangers." We are a team, and therefore we have team support. We can laugh together, plan together, pray together, cry together, and serve the Chief Shepherd together.

I have often sat across from very lonely and hurting pastors during lunch at pastors' conferences. They feel so desperately isolated. I ache inside when I hear their stories. I can't imagine the agony of having no one to turn to. I say to those pastors, "Please pray for Jesus to help you gather a small group around you. Take the initiative, and when you have the group, open up, share your heart, and share your hurt. Receive the prayers of people who can bring God to you. Make friends, perhaps, with another area pastor. Get together regularly and share your life. Talk shop. Pray together."

I remember struggling with a specific memory of a sin I had committed involving an excursion into pornography. I had confessed it totally and honestly to God and had received his forgiveness through the blood of Jesus. Yet the struggle wasn't over. This was one of those sins with which the Enemy continued to needle and accuse me. I needed to obey James 5:16: "Therefore confess your sins *to one another* and pray for one another so that you may be healed." I needed to confess my sin to another believer and be prayed over for healing in my life. Recalling Dr. Victor Matthews's teaching, I knew that confessing my sin *to God* (1 John 1:9) brings *forgiveness* through the blood of Christ for the *act(s)* of sin. Confessing my sin face to face with *another person* (James 5:16) brings *healing* through the power of the Spirit to the inner brokenness and *lie* that serves as the *trigger* of sin. Also, I knew that if I obeyed James 5:16, the devil's accusing hold on me would be broken.

A Vineyard pastor and good friend from another town came to see me, and we were updating one another about our lives and ministries. As we talked, I felt the Spirit prompt me with, "This is the time and this is the person. Get it done."

"Oh, Lord, no. What will he think if I tell him? I will be so humiliated. Lord, I'm scared."

The Spirit pressed in, "This is the time. Do it."

I told my pastor-friend that I needed to get something out of the darkness of my soul and into the light. I wanted to obey James 5:16. My friend listened patiently and well. Feeling awkward and embarrassed, I told him the dark and guilt-soaked story.

When I finished, he smiled at me. He told me that he loved me and respected me. Then he said, "John, based upon your confession, I, with all the authority of God given to me by his Holy Spirit, declare you forgiven of your specific and confessed sin."

On hearing his words, something deep inside me felt like it clicked, like a tumbler in the massive door of a safe falling into place, like a crucial alignment being made in my soul. Not only did the freedom of forgiveness flood my soul, not only did I sense Satan's grip broken, I perceived that the area of my soul that made me vulnerable to that particular sinful experience was touched in some life-changing way. I had done my part in obedience to James 5:16, and, thank God, he did his part! Yet—and this is the point—God had done it through another person. Another pastor pastored me.

MEETING JESUS IN NEW WAYS

In allowing ourselves to be pastored by others, we will find ourselves meeting Jesus in ways that will refresh and renew our lives. Of course, the people we invite into our lives must be people we can trust. Jesus, the overseer of your soul, knows the people with whom you need to connect. If you are a lonely shepherd, with God's help find them.

The elder who left the church after I wrote him that I could no longer meet with him for breakfast went off to another church in town. There the Lord met him in renewing ways. The way he tells it now, he too "hit the wall" and realized how he had gotten off base in his views of God, the church, and leadership. Some years later, he and his family came back to our church. He and I did the Larry Crabb thing: we (re)connected. Because God had been meeting and transforming both of us, we were able to reflect back on those turbulent morning meetings with new perspectives.

We talked, recalling the past breakdown in our relationship. He admitted to me that he held back then a "model" of leadership that did not fit my spiritual gifts or me. He was well intentioned but misguided in trying to shoehorn me into a pattern that I did not fit. He had been very frustrated with me.

I admitted to him that I had no inner strength at the time to tell him that his earnest attempts to make me a better leader were actually killing me inside. It wasn't his fault that I did not speak up and say, "No. This is not working. I am not *that kind* of leader." We acknowledged our errors, admitted our wounded feelings, and forgave one another from the heart. We now serve together again on the elder council.

Jesus, our Chief Shepherd, on his scariest night—the night he was betrayed and arrested—invited his closest friends into his struggle. "Watch with me and pray with me," he asked (see Mark 14:32–42). If Jesus invited that kind of support and modeled that kind of vulnerability, how much more do we need to be like him?

Pastors, brothers and sisters in Christ, let us grow in our calling to bring God to people. Let's seek greater empowerment from the Spirit for our lives and for the people in our charge. Let's ask for more of the Spirit to accomplish our task. "The future belongs to the Spirit."[3] For the sake of the Father's glory, in the name above all names—Jesus Christ, and by the power of the Holy Spirit, may we keep on discovering the thrill and challenge of becoming like and serving under Jesus Christ.

God used a brief, turbulent conversation on a tour bus in India to plant some seeds in me that have blossomed into this extended conversation with you. My hope is that a thought or two—even if you tend to disagree with them—will lodge in your thinking and result in a bountiful harvest for you personally and for your ministry. Remember concerning our differences that the blade sharpens even as the sparks fly.

A few words penned in my copy of *Five Smooth Stones for Pastoral Work* launched me into serious reflection and fascinating discovery about Jesus as the model of pastoral ministry. Jesus is the Kings of Kings. True. He is the Lord of Lords. Right. I hope you have grown to love him more, trust him more, and be like him more as the Pastor of Pastors—Jesus, the Great Shepherd of the sheep.

For John,

Sharing the life of Christ in the work of pastor. . . .

Eugene H. Peterson

NOTES

INTRODUCTION—JESUS: THE MISSING PASTOR

1. J. Jeremias, "Poimen," in *Theological Dictionary of the New Testament*, ed. G. Kittel and G. Friedrich, trans. G. Bromiley (Grand Rapids: Eerdmans, 1968), 6:485–502. "The shepherd is never judged adversely in the NT. . . . The *high estimation of the shepherd* in all this stands in such striking contrast to the contempt of the Rabbis that one is forced to conclude that it mirrors directly *the actuality of the life of Jesus*, who had fellowship with the despised and sinners, and who shared sympathetically their life" (p. 490, italics mine).

2. David Fisher, *The 21st-Century Pastor: A Vision Based on the Ministry of Paul* (Grand Rapids: Zondervan, 1996). While much of Fisher's book is helpful to me, I am still puzzled by the primarily Pauline definitions for ministry. While affirming Fisher's commendable contribution to understanding pastoral ministry, I attempt simply to expand on what Fisher himself acknowledges when he writes, "In Romans 1, Paul links his apostolic ministry to the person of Christ. Likewise, all Christian calling must be centered in Christ" (p. 97). My aim is to express the centrality of Christ in pastoral, not apostolic, ministry.

CHAPTER 1—JESUS THE PASTOR

1. Louis Goldberg, *bin* ("understanding") in *Theological Wordbook of the Old Testament*, ed. R. Laird Harris, Gleason L. Archer Jr., and Bruce K. Waltke (Chicago: Moody Press, 1980), 1:103–4.

2. Oswald Chambers, *My Utmost for His Highest: An Updated Edition in Today's Language*, ed. James Reimann (Grand Rapids: Discovery House, 1992), devotion for January 20.

3. I first heard Victor Matthews say something to this effect in a class-room, and his words stuck with me. I have heard him say them in other teaching situations since then.

4. Eugene H. Peterson, *The Contemplative Pastor* (Dallas: Word, 1989), 117–22. "If we avoid small talk, we abandon the very field in which we have been assigned to work" (p. 121).

5. Eugene H. Peterson, *Leap Over a Wall: Earthly Spirituality for Everyday Christians: Reflections on the Life of David* (San Francisco: HarperSanFrancisco, 1997), 3: "Story is the primary way in which the revelation of God is given to us." Peterson, in *Answering God: The Psalms as Tools for Prayer* (San Francisco: Harper & Row, 1989), 47, writes, "Every life is a story."

6. Leonard Sweet, "A Dream Church for the Twenty-first Century," *The Pastor's Update* 76 (1997), published by Fuller Theological Seminary.

CHAPTER 2—JESUS AND PASTORING

1. Eugene H. Peterson, *Five Smooth Stones for Pastoral Work* (Atlanta: John Knox, 1980). The specific revelation Peterson works with is the Megilloth. From these books Peterson offers captivating descriptions of pastoral work. Some readers of this note may never have considered these Old Testament books as a resource for crafting a pastoral vision. The Megilloth includes Ruth, Esther, Ecclesiastes, Song of Songs, and Lamentations.

2. Ibid., 14.

3. Derek J. Tidball, *Skillful Shepherds: An Introduction to Pastoral Theology* (Grand Rapids: Zondervan, 1986), 77.

4. Everett F. Harrison, *A Short Life of Christ* (Grand Rapids: Eerdmans, 1968), 61.

5. Tidball, *Skillful Shepherds*, 56.

6. David Fisher, *The 21st-Century Pastor: A Vision Based on the Ministry of Paul* (Grand Rapids: Zondervan, 1996), 159–73, presents a compelling discussion of "the pastor's heart" based on Paul's use of the father/mother metaphors.

7. I heard this definition of pastoring from Don Cousins, a church con-sultant and former staff member of Willow Creek Community Church, South Barrington, Illinois. For me it was a simple yet profound definition.

CHAPTER 3—JESUS AND PROMISE

1. Helmut Thielicke, "Beyond Pushing and Producing," *Leadership Journal,* Fall 1995, 85.

2. R. T. France, *Jesus and the Old Testament: His Application of the Old Testament to Himself and His Mission* (London: Tyndale, 1971), 223.

3. Christopher J. H. Wright, *Knowing Jesus Through the Old Testament* (Grand Rapids: Marshall Pickering, 1992), 108.

4. Douglas D. Webster, *A Passion for Christ: An Evangelical Christology* (Grand Rapids: Zondervan, 1987), 96. Webster, in his excellent contribution to Christology, continually presses the question of Christian transformation. I heartily recommend his work to Christians, especially pastors, who long to be more like Jesus. Sadly, I think his book is out of print.

5. Eugene H. Peterson, *Run with the Horses: The Quest for Life at Its Best* (Downers Grove, Ill.: InterVarsity Press, 1983), 25.

6. C. S. Lewis, *That Hideous Strength* (New York: Macmillan, 1946), 318–19. The full description of Jane's conversion is a startling and creative portrayal of being "born from above" (see John 3).

7. Eugene H. Peterson, *Five Smooth Stones for Pastoral Work* (Atlanta: John Knox, 1980), 80.

8. A. W. Tozer, *The Knowledge of the Holy: The Attributes of God and Their Meaning in the Christian Life* (New York: Harper & Row, 1961), 66.

9. Larry Crabb Jr., *Finding God* (Grand Rapids: Zondervan, 1993), 104.

10. Michael Riddell, *Threshold of the Future: Reforming the Church in the Post-Christian West* (London: SPCK, 1998), 82–83.

11. Webster, *Passion for Christ,* 89.

CHAPTER 4—JESUS AND THE SPIRIT

1. Gerald F. Hawthorne, *The Power and the Presence: The Significance of the Holy Spirit in the Life and Ministry of Jesus* (Dallas: Word, 1991), 148.

2. Ibid., 35.

CHAPTER 5—JESUS AND HIS YOKE

1. Hans-Georg Link, "Yoke," in *The New International Dictionary of New Testament Theology*, ed. Colin Brown, 3 vols. (Grand Rapids: Zondervan, 1986), 3:1163, points out that taking Jesus' "yoke" is not only accepting his teaching, but imitating the virtues that characterized Jesus' life.

2. John Ortberg, *Love Beyond Reason: Moving God's Love from Your Head to Your Heart* (Grand Rapids: Zondervan, 1998), presents a delightful discussion of this vital and life-changing reality.

3. Ibid., 14.

4. A. W. Tozer, *The Pursuit of God* (Harrisburg, Pa.: Christian Publications, 1958), 64.

CHAPTER 6—JESUS AND COMPASSION

1. Thomas C. Oden, *Care of Souls in the Classic Tradition* (Philadelphia: Fortress Press, 1984), is an excellent and stimulating reminder for pastors of the high calling to "soul care." Oden's discussion points to reasons why our theological training is deficient in sustaining the art of curing souls. The secular triumph of psychological therapy severed ministers from their ministry-shaping, pastoral roots.

2. Comments about my seminary training are not given with even a hint of disrespect. I thank God frequently for the biblical and theological grounding I received at both the Moody Bible Institute and Dallas Theological Seminary. This story is about my personal and pastoral journey and how I have explored beliefs and practices that were not affirmed as defensible *within the theological system* of those who taught me. The transitions that I have made in theological understanding and pastoral practice are not meant, however, to reflect negatively on the people who taught me and places where I was taught.

3. See articles referenced in nn. 7 and 9 below for these definitions.

4. I understand that there is a textual variant in Mark 1:35. Some early manuscripts read "anger" instead of "compassion." Either way, the emotion is strong and provokes merciful intervention by Jesus. See William Lane, *Mark*, New International Commentary on the New Testament (Grand Rapids: Eerdmans, 1994), 84, for a good discussion of the textual variant.

5. Donald B. Kraybill, *The Upside Down Kingdom*, rev. ed. (Scottdale, Pa.: Herald, 1990). Kraybill's analysis of the cultural dynamics involved in Jesus' conversation with the woman at the well has shaped my thinking immensely, for which I am truly grateful.

6. Lee Strobel, *What Jesus Would Say* (Grand Rapids: Zondervan, 1994), 24–25.

7. Hans-Helmut Esser, "Compassion," in *The New International Dictionary of New Testament Theology*, ed. Colin Brown (Grand Rapids: Zondervan, 1978), 2:600.

8. W. D. Davies and Dale C. Allison Jr., *A Critical and Exegetical Commentary on the Gospel According to Saint Matthew* (Edinburgh: T. & T. Clark, 1991), 2:147, n. 13.

9. Helmut Kosser, "Splanchnizomai," in *Theological Dictionary of the New Testament*, ed. G. Kittel and G. Friedrich, trans. G. Bromiley (Grand Rapids, Eerdmans, 1975), 7:556. It is very instructive that Paul viewed his bonding to Jesus Christ, captured in his phrase "in Christ," as the origin of his totally compelling love for others. Paul felt deeply for others, but the source of his compassion was Christ.

10. Dallas Willard, *The Divine Conspiracy: Rediscovering Our Hidden Life in God* (San Francisco: HarperSanFrancisco, 1998), 301.

11. Henri J. M. Nouwen, *The Way of the Heart: Desert Spirituality and Contemporary Ministry* (San Francisco: HarperCollins, 1981), 24.

12. Eugene H. Peterson, *Five Smooth Stones for Pastoral Work* (Atlanta: John Knox, 1980), 73.

13. Eugene H. Peterson, *Run with the Horses: The Quest for Life at Its Best* (Downers Grove, Ill.: InterVarsity Press, 1983), 80.

14. Kenneth E. Bailey, *Poet and Peasant: A Literary-Cultural Approach to the Parables of Luke* (Grand Rapids: Eerdmans, 1983), 143.

CHAPTER 7—JESUS AND THE SPIRITUAL DISCIPLINES

1. Dallas Willard, *The Spirit of the Disciplines: Understanding How God Changes Lives* (New York: Harper & Row, 1988), 264.

2. John R. W. Stott, *Understanding Christ: An Inquiry into the Theology of Prepositions* (Grand Rapids: Zondervan, 1979), 142.

3. Gunther Ebel, "Peripateo," in *The New International Dictionary of New Testament Theology*, ed. Colin Brown (Grand Rapids: Zondervan, 1978), 3:943–45.

4. Glenn W. Barker, "1 John" in *The Expositor's Bible Commentary*, ed. Frank Gaebelein (Grand Rapids: Zondervan, 1981), 12:316.

5. John Ortberg, *Love Beyond Reason: Moving God's Love from Your Head to Your Heart* (Grand Rapids: Zondervan, 1998), 79.

6. Dallas Willard, *The Divine Conspiracy: Rediscovering Our Hidden Life in God* (San Francisco: HarperSanFrancisco, 1998), 283. Willard writes, "I am not necessarily learning to do everything he did, but I am learning to do everything I do in the manner that he did all that he did." Willard defines a disciple as one who lives the way Jesus would live if Jesus were in his or her place.

7. That Jesus practiced the disciplines as a Spirit-empowered human being is demonstrated in the Gospels. I suggest the following references in Luke as illustrative, not exhaustive: fasting, 4:2; prayer and solitude, 5:16; service, 22:27; submission, 22:42; and meditation, chapter 15 (the stories of the lost sheep, lost coin, and lost son). Jesus' creative use of imagination to convey the kingdom of God in stories illustrates his keen meditative discipline.

8. I have found these three books excellent resources on the subject of the spiritual disciplines: Richard Foster, *Celebration of Discipline* (San Francisco: Harper & Row, 1978); John Ortberg, *The Life You've Always Wanted: Spiritual Discipline for Ordinary People* (Grand Rapids: Zondervan, 1997); and Dallas Willard's books *The Spirit of the Disciplines* and *The Divine Conspiracy.* Also very helpful and practical is Douglas Rumford's *Soulshaping: Taking Care of Your Spiritual Life Through Godly Disciplines* (Wheaton, Ill.: Tyndale House, 1996).

9. Willard, *Spirit of the Disciplines,* ix.

10. Dallas Willard, *In Search of Guidance: Developing a Conversational Relationship with God* (Ventura, Calif.: Regal, 1984), 19.

11. Leanne Payne, *Listening Prayer: Learning to Hear God's Voice and Keep a Prayer Journal* (Grand Rapids: Baker, 1994), 124.

12. A. W. Tozer, *The Pursuit of God* (Harrisburg, Pa.: Christian Publications, 1958), 74.

13. Willard, *Spirit of the Disciplines,* 161.

14. John Ortberg, "What's Really Behind Our Fatigue," *Leadership Journal,* Spring 1997, 112.

15. Eugene H. Peterson, *The Contemplative Pastor* (Dallas: Word, 1989), 33.

16. Jack Deere, *Surprised by the Power of the Spirit: A Former Dallas Seminary Pro-*

fessor Discovers That God Still Speaks and Heals Today (Grand Rapids: Zondervan, 1993), 187, 191.

17. Scotty Smith and Michael Card, *Unveiled Hope: Eternal Encouragement from the Book of Revelation* (Nashville: Thomas Nelson, 1997), 87–88.

18. Henri J. M. Nouwen, *The Return of the Prodigal Son: Meditations on Fathers, Brothers and Sons* (New York: Doubleday, 1992), 90: "As Father, the only authority he claims for himself is the authority of compassion."

CHAPTER 8—JESUS AS PASTOR-TEACHER

1. Leonard Sweet, *SoulTsunami: Sink or Swim in New Millennium Culture* (Grand Rapids: Zondervan, 1999), 411.

2. An excellent (though dated) presentation of Jesus as Teacher is Herman Harrell Horne's *Jesus: The Master Teacher* (Grand Rapids: Kregel, 1964).

3. Jim Cymbala, *Fresh Wind, Fresh Fire: What Happens When God's Spirit Invades the Hearts of His People* (Grand Rapids: Zondervan, 1997), 150–51.

4. John Ortberg, *Love Beyond Reason: Moving God's Love from Your Head to Your Heart* (Grand Rapids: Zondervan, 1998), 79.

CHAPTER 9—JESUS AND SPIRITUAL CONFLICT

1. David Damico, *The Faces of Rage: Resolving the Losses That Lead to Anger, Guilt, Shame, Cynicism, Isolation, Compulsions, Pretense, Legalism, Perfectionism* (Colorado Springs: NavPress, 1992). This book, suggested by my counselor, helped me in layperson's terms to "interpret" the losses in my past. Discovering that the wild dynamics of my inner life in my early forties were not immoral or unspiritual, but simply evidentiary of brokenness, brought tremendous healing and freedom.

2. C. Fred Dickason, *Demon Possession and the Christian* (Chicago: Moody Press, 1987). Dickason, a dispensational cessationist, perceptively speaks about spiritual powers and about the need for the church to make spiritual warfare an intentional aspect of Christian living and pastoral/local church ministry.

3. Timothy M. Warner, *Spiritual Warfare: Victory over the Powers of This Dark World* (Wheaton, Ill.: Crossway, 1991).

4. Neil Anderson, *The Bondage Breaker* (Eugene, Ore.: Harvest House, 1990).

5. Clinton E. Arnold, *Three Crucial Questions About Spiritual Warfare* (Grand Rapids: Baker, 1997). Arnold's opening chapter, "What Is Spiritual Warfare?" is profound and offers a biblically balanced introduction to those unfamiliar with the subject.

6. D. Martin Lloyd-Jones, *The Christian Warfare: An Exposition of Ephesians 6:10–13* (Grand Rapids: Baker, 1976).

7. Ibid., 19.

8. Neil Anderson and Charles Mylander, *Setting Your Church Free* (Ventura, Calif.: Regal, 1994), 128.

9. William Lane, *Mark*, New International Commentary on the New Testament (Grand Rapids: Eerdmans, 1994), 179–89. Lane's discussion of this text bristles with insight for understanding and engaging in spiritual warfare. Lane presents the parallel between Mark 4:35–41 (the stilling of the storm) and Mark 5:1–20 (the exorcising of "Legion" from the Gadarene demoniac). Lane's commentary on Mark's gospel exhibits diligent research and is pastorally profound.

10. Neil Anderson's training seminar called "Seven Steps to Freedom" is both thoroughly biblical and readily practical. The Seven Steps material helps people discover, define, and renounce any lies of the Enemy that may be holding them in bondage. Anderson's book *The Bondage Breaker* explains the teaching and methodology of the Seven Steps.

11. An alert reader might ask, "In what way?" That is a good question, and I simply refer the reader to the works of leaders like C. Fred Dickason, Timothy M. Warner, Neil Anderson, Clinton E. Arnold, and Leanne Payne for the actual practice of warfare in the spiritual realm.

CHAPTER 10—COLLABORATORS WITH JESUS

1. Saint Augustine, *Confessions*, trans. Henry Chadock (New York: Oxford University Press, 1991), 183.

CHAPTER 11—JESUS AND HIS SPIRIT-EMPOWERED CHURCH

1. John Naisbitt and Patricia Aburdene, *Megatrends 2000: Ten New Directions for the 1990s* (New York: William Morrow, 1990), 271–72.

2. D. A. Carson, *Showing the Spirit: A Theological Exposition of 1 Corinthians 12–14* (Grand Rapids: Baker, 1987), 110. In this section of his book, Carson is

discussing the cessationist's interpretation of Paul's use of Isaiah 28:11–12 in 1 Corinthians 14:20–25. Carson states, "Second, some writers of dispensational persuasion say that Paul's point in quoting the passage from Isaiah is to affirm that tongues are a sign exclusively for *Jewish* people. . . . The exegetical naivete is somewhat staggering and turns in part on how the New Testament writers use the Old Testament."

3. John A. MacArthur Jr., *Charismatic Chaos* (Grand Rapids: Zondervan, 1992). I respect MacArthur as a prominent Christian leader, and I have benefited from his ministry, yet I am deeply disappointed in the tabloid nature of this book. He seems to have deliberately selected the most bizarre examples of what he considers dangerous to sound biblical doctrine (his views) and practice (his ways).

4. Gerald F. Hawthorne, *The Power and the Presence: The Significance of the Holy Spirit in the Life and Ministry of Jesus* (Dallas: Word, 1991), 238.

5. Dallas Willard, *In Search of Guidance: Developing a Conversational Relationship with God* (Ventura, Calif.: Regal, 1984), 127.

6. Charles Swindoll, "Dallas's New Dispensation," *Christianity Today*, October 25, 1993, 14.

7. Charles Stanley, *The Wonderful Spirit-Filled Life* (Nashville: Thomas Nelson, 1992), 179.

8. Daniel B. Wallace, "Who's Afraid of the Holy Spirit?" *Christianity Today*, September 12, 1994, 37.

9. Frederick Dale Bruner, *A Theology of the Holy Spirit: The Pentecostal Experience and the New Testament Witness* (Grand Rapids: Eerdmans, 1970), 128–29. Bruner writes, "On receiving Christ there should be no more thirsting after 'deeper' spiritual experiences as though the water faith receives from Christ is not entirely satisfying and empowering" (pp. 254–55). "There is no such 'more'" (p. 244). While I appreciate Bruner's presentation of the exegetical flaws of Pentecostal theology, the idea that Christians of any persuasion need no more of God is astounding. If I am finite and God is infinite, I will eternally be receiving more of who God is. Pentecostals simply call us to start receiving more of God now.

10. Walter Brueggemann, *The Message of the Psalms: A Theological Commentary*, Augsburg Old Testament Studies (Minneapolis: Augsburg, 1984), 111.

11. Charles Ryrie, "The Holy Spirit: God at Work," *Christianity Today*, March 19, 1990, 33.

12. Some New Testament scholars note that the Spirit's working miracles among the Galatian believers is parallel to the manifestations of the Spirit's power in the Corinthian church. The *church*, not just the apostles, was the recipient of gifts of power. See, e.g., Richard N. Longenecker, *Galatians*, Word Biblical Commentary (Dallas: Word, 1990), 105, who comments on Galatians 3:5, "*Dunameis* ('miracles') refers to outward manifestations of the Spirit's presence such as enumerated in 1 Cor. 12:7–11 . . . *humin* . . . means 'among you' . . . and so refers to the Galatians themselves as the recipients of the Spirit's charismatic activities."

13. Gordon D. Fee, *The First Epistle to the Corinthians*, New International Commentary on the New Testament (Grand Rapids: Eerdmans, 1987), 582.

14. Wayne Grudem, *Systematic Theology: An Introduction to Biblical Doctrine* (Grand Rapids: Zondervan, 1994).

15. See D. A. Carson, *Showing the Spirit: A Theological Exposition of 1 Corinthians 12–14* (Grand Rapids: Baker, 1987), 108–17, and Fee, *The First Epistle to the Corinthians*, 678–88.

16. Jack Deere, *Surprised by the Power of the Spirit: A Former Dallas Seminary Professor Discovers That God Still Speaks and Heals Today* (Grand Rapids: Zondervan, 1993), 229–52.

17. Derek J. Tidball, *Skillful Shepherds: An Introduction to Pastoral Theology* (Grand Rapids: Zondervan, 1986), 337.

18. Wayne Grudem, *The Gift of Prophecy in the New Testament and Today* (Westchester, Ill.: Crossway, 1988), 14. In his *Systematic Theology*, Grudem more precisely states that New Testament "prophecy occurs when a revelation from God is reported in the prophet's own (merely human) words" (p. 1057).

19. Charles Swindoll, "Helping and the Holy Spirit: An Interview with Chuck Swindoll," *Christian Counseling Today*, Winter 1994, 17.

20. Sally Morgenthaler, *Worship Evangelism* (Grand Rapids: Zondervan, 1995), 84.

CHAPTER 12—JESUS AND COMMUNITY

1. Larry Crabb, *Connecting: A Radical New Vision* (Nashville: Word, 1997), 43, 45.

2. In a little, self-published book called *God Guides*, Mary Geegh tells many fascinating stories of God's responses to listening prayer. A former mis-

sionary to India, Mary Geegh passed away in Holland, Michigan, in January 1999 at the age of 101. The book can be obtained by writing to her nephew, Samuel Geegh, at 6325 Lakeshore Drive, West Olive, MI 49460.

3. This is a phrase I heard John Ortberg of Willow Creek Church use. It offers hope and an invitation to trust the Spirit for great things in our lives and ministries.

Time Saving Ideas for

YOUR CHURCH SIGN

1001 Attention-Getting Sayings

Veryln D. Verbrugge

Signs have been almost as much a part of the modern church as the front doors. For that matter, they've been the entry into church life for countless people who have responded to their brief but cogent message. Your church sign has more potential than you may imagine—if you're smart in using it.

Your Church Sign offers you sound pointers on signage. You'll find tips on impactful sign placement, captions, themes, and how to write effective messages. And you'll get more than one thousand ready-made, eye-catching sayings. Some are humorous, some are encouraging, some are wise, some are convicting. All are designed to turn scant seconds of drive-by time into active spiritual awareness.

Arranged by theme, *Your Church Sign* offers captions on:

Marriage and the Family	God in Charge
Prayer	Evangelism
Going to Church	The Bible
Seasonal Themes	Speech
Christian Living	…and more

Turn to this practical, easy-to-use book for fast ideas and proven advice for helping your church sign make a difference in people's lives.

Softcover ISBN 0-310-22802-6

"Tender your heart well; it is God's garden."

"It wasn't the apple on the tree. It was the pair beneath."

"Good-byes are the law of Earth, reunions the law of Heaven."

Pick up a copy today at your favorite bookstore!

ZONDERVAN™

GRAND RAPIDS, MICHIGAN 49530 USA

WWW.ZONDERVAN.COM

THE PURPOSE-DRIVEN® CHURCH

Growth Without Compromising Your Message and Mission

Rick Warren

Cross the bridge between the church you are and the church you want to be

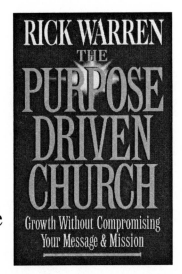

Read the groundbreaking half-million-copy best-seller that has influenced churches worldwide. This award-winning book offers a biblical and practical strategy to empower churches to minister to the 21st century. Rick Warren, pastor of Saddleback Valley Community Church, demonstrates that growing churches have a clear-cut identity and mission, precise in their purpose and knowing what God has called them to do.

Hardcover ISBN 0-310-20106-3
Audio Pages® Abridged Cassettes ISBN 0-310-20518-2
Abridged Audio CD ISBN 0-310-25988-6

Pick up a copy today at your favorite bookstore!

ZONDERVAN™

GRAND RAPIDS, MICHIGAN 49530 USA

WWW.ZONDERVAN.COM

TRANSITIONING

Leading Your Church
Through Change

Dan Southerland

If you've been thinking about leading your traditional church toward becoming a purpose-driven church, *Transitioning* gives you the wisdom and guidance you need. Drawing from a wealth of experience, pastor Dan Southerland takes you through the eight-step process of discovering and implementing God's unique mission for your congregation. With thought, prayer, planning, and patience, you and your church can discover the rich rewards of being purpose-driven.

"One of the most exciting and encouraging examples of transitioning from being program driven to purpose driven."

— From the foreword by Rick Warren, Author of *The Purpose-Driven®* *Church*

Softcover: ISBN 0-310-24268-1

Pick up a copy today at your favorite bookstore!

GRAND RAPIDS, MICHIGAN 49530 USA

WWW.ZONDERVAN.COM

THE WORD AND POWER CHURCH

What Happens When a Church Seeks All God Has to Offer?

Doug Banister

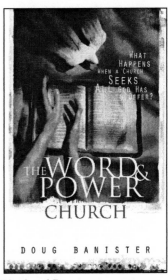

Like spiritual Hatfields and McCoys, evangelicals and charismatics have long been trading salvos over the doctrinal wall. One side has championed the Word; the other, the Holy Spirit. But are the Word and the Spirit really in conflict? Or has God's ideal, all along, included both? The Truth and the Spirit. Sound biblical teaching and God's leading. The Word and Power.

Filled with personal anecdotes, this fascinating, thought-provoking, and candid book supplies the why-to's and how-to's of a Word-and-Power approach. What you won't find is preferential treatment of one view over another. What you will find are thoughtful biblical insights that will challenge you and inspire you. And you'll discover practical guidance for charting your course—whether as an individual or as a church—toward a faith that embraces the truth of the Word and the power of the Spirit.

Today, more and more Christians are realizing that it's time for us to lay down our weapons and embrace the strengths each side has to offer. Time to become what God has always intended us to be: *The Word and Power Church.*

Softcover ISBN 0-310-24267-3

Pick up a copy today at your favorite bookstore!

GRAND RAPIDS, MICHIGAN 49530 USA

WWW.ZONDERVAN.COM

THE 21ST CENTURY PASTOR

A Vision Based on the Ministry of Paul

David Fisher

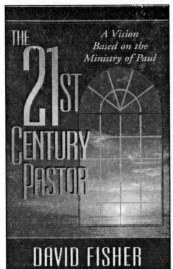

With 25 years of pastoral experience, David Fisher recognizes and deals with the struggles pastors experience at various times throughout a ministry, including identity crisis and unrealistic expectations of congregations.

Using Paul's pastoral metaphors, Fisher paints a portrait of the 21st century minister able to survive his world. According to Paul, the pastor's role as Christ's penmen gives him the "opportunity to write the larger story of God's purpose for the universe." In a similar way, God has called pastors to act as ambassadors to the world-proud deliverers of God's authority.

While applying Paul's metaphors, Fisher says it is imperative for the postmodern church and pastor to love one another, promote integrity, and develop unity and faithfulness.

In order to find God's success, Fisher recommends pastors define who they are in Christ, know the immediate culture, and discover how the church should operate in the postmodern era.

"Paul uses a metaphor to describe how God's preachers bear his glory: 'We have this treasure in jars of clay' (2 Cor. 4:7)," says Fisher. "To put it in more contemporary language, God does his divine work through fallen, fallible, and sinful human instruments. God puts the gospel in clay pots that crack and break."

Softcover ISBN 0-310-20154-3

Pick up a copy today at your favorite bookstore!

GRAND RAPIDS, MICHIGAN 49530 USA

WWW.ZONDERVAN.COM

THE OTHER SIDE OF PASTORAL MINISTRY

Using Process Leadership to Transform Your Church

Daniel A. Brown

Daniel Brown believes churches ought to flow like a river, not sit motionless like a lake. A veteran pastor, Brown knows that River Churches are alive, dynamic, gaining momentum, changing courses. He also knows the power such churches can have to change lives.

In *The Other Side of Pastoral Ministry,* he shows what makes a River Church flow and invites pastors and church leaders to follow ten key "currents" that can move their people to new places of faith and service. Brown reveals the crucial dynamics of:

* Building authority
* Defining and communicating vision
* Strengthening systems
* Coaxing changes
* Empowering people for ministry
* Adjusting church culture
* Positioning and unleashing resources
* Maintaining identity
* Understanding the times
* Evaluating results

If you're ready for a church whose focus is on involvement, not attendance on "What happened to the people who showed up?" not "How many showed up?" then this insightful, anecdote-filled book will provide you with practical suggestions and thought-patterns to move into the flow of the River.

Softcover ISBN 0-310-20602-2

Pick up a copy today at your favorite bookstore!

ZONDERVAN™

GRAND RAPIDS, MICHIGAN 49530 USA

WWW.ZONDERVAN.COM

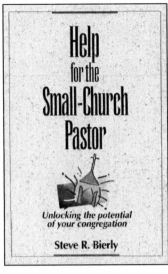

HELP FOR THE SMALL-CHURCH PASTOR

Unlocking the Potential of Your Congregation

Steve R. Bierly

Churches of fewer than 150 remain the rule rather than the exception in American Christianity. However, seminaries don't equip students in every way that's necessary to lead smaller congregations effectively—despite the fact that most seminary graduates will become small-church pastors.

Help for the Small-Church Pastor offers pastors of small churches the guidance and encouragement they need. In this common-sense book, Steve Bierly draws from his many years in ministry to show what makes smaller congregations tick.

Softcover ISBN 0-310-49951-8

Pick up a copy today at your favorite bookstore!

ZONDERVAN™

GRAND RAPIDS, MICHIGAN 49530 USA

WWW.ZONDERVAN.COM

How to Thrive as a Small-Church Pastor

A Guide to Spiritual and Emotional Well-Being

Steve R. Bierly

Steve Bierly knows firsthand the needs and concerns of small-church pastors. He also knows how to meet the needs, handle the concerns, and thrive as a pastor with a congregation of 150 or less.

Drawing on his twelve years of small-church experience, Bierly helps pastors reframe their perspective of God, ministry, relationships, their own needs, and more. He offers seasoned, fatherly counsel—assurance to small-church pastors that they're not alone; a fresh outlook on the successes of their ministries; and an upbeat, practical approach to spiritual, emotional, and physical well-being.

Filled with good humor, here is help for small-church pastors to face the rigors of their vocation realistically and reclaim their first love of ministry.

Softcover ISBN 0-310-21655-9

Pick up a copy today at your favorite bookstore!

PREACHING THAT CONNECTS

Using the Techniques of Journalists to Add
Impact to Your Sermons

Mark Galli
& Craig Brian Larson

Master the craft of effective communication that grabs attention and wins hearts

Like everyone else, preachers long to be understood. Unfortunately the rules first learned in seminary, if misapplied, can quickly turn homiletic precision into listener boredom.

To capture the heart and mind, Mark Galli and Craig Brian Larson suggest preachers turn to the lessons of journalism. In *Preaching that Connects* they show how the same keys used to create effective, captivating communication in the media can transform a sermon.

Amply illustrated from some of today's best preachers, *Preaching that Connects* walks through the entire sermon, from the critical introduction, to the bridge, to illustrations and final application. Key points include the five key techniques for generating creative ideas, your six options for illustrations, and the ten rules for great story-telling—and why the transition sentence is the hardest sentence you'll write.

Preaching that Connects is for all who seek to hone their craft to communicate the truth of the Gospel effectively.

Softcover ISBN 0-310-38621-7

Pick up a copy today at your favorite bookstore!

GRAND RAPIDS, MICHIGAN 49530 USA

WWW.ZONDERVAN.COM

Preaching With Purpose

The Urgent Task of Homiletics

Jay E. Adams

"The amazing lack of concern for purpose among homileticians and preachers has spawned a brood of preachers who are dull, lifeless, abstract, and impersonal; it has obscured truth, hindered joyous Christian living, destroyed dedication and initiative, and stifled service for Christ." (from chapter 1 of *Preaching With Purpose*)

Preaching needs to become purposeful, says Jay Adams, because purposeless preaching is deadly. This book was written to help preachers and students of preaching to discover the purpose that preaching has and the ways that the Scriptures inform and direct the preaching task.

Preaching With Purpose, like the many other books by Jay Adams, speaks clearly and forcefully to the issue. Having read this book, both students and experienced preachers will be unable to ignore the urgent task of purposeful preaching. And the people of God will be the better for it.

Softcover ISBN 0-310-51091-0

Pick up a copy today at your favorite bookstore!

GRAND RAPIDS, MICHIGAN 49530 USA

WWW.ZONDERVAN.COM

We want to hear from you. Please send your comments about this book to us in care of the address below. Thank you.

GRAND RAPIDS, MICHIGAN 49530 USA
WWW.ZONDERVAN.COM